Bruno Tertrais

Nuclear Policies
in Europe

Adelphi Paper 327

Oxford University Press, Great Clarendon Street, Oxford OX2 6DP
Oxford New York
Athens Auckland Bangkok Bombay Calcutta Cape Town
Dar es Salaam Delhi Florence Hong Kong Istanbul Karachi
Kuala Lumpur Madras Madrid Melbourne Mexico City
Nairobi Paris Singapore Taipei Tokyo Toronto
and associated companies in
Berlin Ibadan

Oxford is a trade mark of Oxford University Press

Published in the United States
by Oxford University Press Inc., New York

© International Institute for Strategic Studies 1999

First published March 1999 by **Oxford University Press** for
International Institute for Strategic Studies
23 Tavistock Street, London WC2E 7NQ   ·

Director John Chipman
Editor Gerald Segal
Assistant Editor Matthew Foley
Design and Production Mark Taylor

British Library Cataloguing in Publication Data
Data available

Library of Congress Cataloguing in Publication Data

ISBN 0-19-922427-7
ISSN 0567-932x

contents

glossary

ABM	Anti-Ballistic Missile
ASMP	*Air-Sol, Moyenne Portée*
AWACS	airborne warning and control system
CFE	Conventional Armed Forces in Europe
CTBT	Comprehensive Test Ban Treaty
DGP	Senior Defence Group on Proliferation (NATO)
EMU	Economic and Monetary Union
EU	European Union
Euratom	European Atomic Energy Community
G-8	Group of Eight industrial nations
GAO	General Accounting Office (US)
GDR	German Democratic Republic
HLG	High Level Group (NATO)
IAEA	International Atomic Energy Agency
ICBM	intercontinental ballistic missile
ICJ	International Court of Justice
INF	Intermediate-range Nuclear Forces
IRBM	intermediate-range ballistic missile
MIRV	multiple independently targetable re-entry vehicle
NAC	North Atlantic Council (NATO)
NBC	nuclear, biological and chemical

NGO	non-governmental organisation
NMD	National Missile Defense
NPG	Nuclear Planning Group
NPT	Nuclear Non-Proliferation Treaty
NSA	negative security assurance
OSCE	Organisation for Security and Cooperation in Europe
PfP	Partnership for Peace (NATO)
PJC	NATO–Russia Permanent Joint Council
PoC	Program of Cooperation (NATO)
PSA	positive security assurance
SAC	Strategic Air Command (US)
SACEUR	Supreme Allied Commander Europe
SDI	Strategic Defense Initiative (US)
SDR	Strategic Defence Review (UK)
SGP	Senior Political–Military Group on Proliferation (NATO)
SHAPE	Supreme Headquarters Allied Powers Europe
SLBM	submarine-launched ballistic missile
SPD	Social Democratic Party (Germany)
SRAM	short-range attack missile
SRBM	short-range ballistic missile
SSBN	nuclear-fuelled ballistic-missile submarine
START	Strategic Arms Reduction Talks
STRATCOM	Strategic Command (US)
USAF	US Air Force
WEU	Western European Union
WMD	weapons of mass destruction

By Cold War standards, Europe has been virtually 'denuclearised'.[1] All former Soviet weapons have been removed from Eastern Europe to Russia, the US maintains only a few hundred warheads in some countries and France and the UK have significantly cut their arsenals. The Czech Republic, Poland and Hungary – which were admitted to NATO in March 1999 – have effectively been denuclearised in advance by the Alliance's declaration in December 1996 that it has 'no intention, no plan and no reason' to base nuclear weapons on their territory.[2] Under the so-called 'Two Plus Four' Treaty of 1990, the former East German *Länder* became the first part of NATO ever to be made a nuclear-weapon-free area by international treaty.

Another, perhaps less noticed, feature of Europe's new nuclear landscape is the gradual harmonisation of doctrines. France, the UK and the US now share the same basic doctrinal principles. No enemy is currently recognised as such, and British, French and US missiles routinely carry no targeting information. Deterrence is addressed 'to whom it may concern', as Sir Michael Quinlan has nicely put it.[3] The dialogue on nuclear policies begun by France and the UK in 1992 has evolved to the point where the two countries now judge that there is no fundamental difference between their doctrines. NATO's collective nuclear needs are now entirely politically driven and, as the Alliance has moved further away from concepts of nuclear war-fighting, reductions have focused attention on issues such as sufficiency and minimal deterrence.

Map 1 *Europe and Nuclear Weapons*

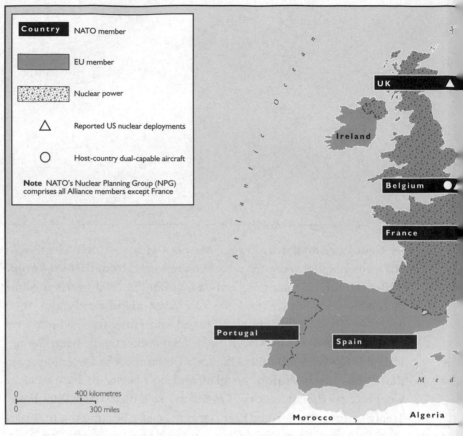

Russian doctrine has also changed.[4] In 1993, Moscow announced that it reserved the right to use nuclear weapons first. In making its position explicit, Russia was at the same time proclaiming negative security assurances (NSAs) – commitments not to use nuclear weapons against non-nuclear countries – that were the same as those of the West. By the same token, the country was also warning any of its neighbours tempted to ally with the West that they would not be immune from Russian nuclear arms. In this way, Moscow was seeking to give coherence to its defence strategy by taking account of its shortcomings in conventional weaponry. The fundamental Cold War asymmetry – Eastern conventional super-

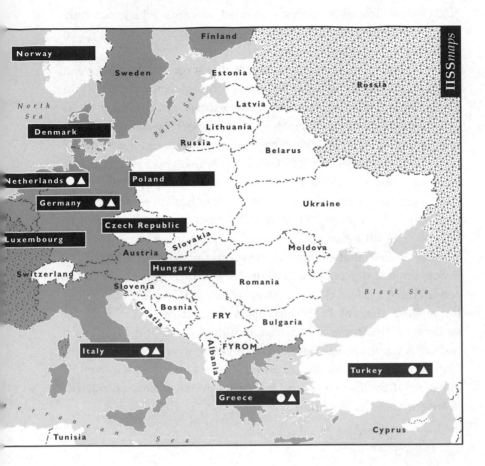

iority balanced by the West's reliance on nuclear weapons – has been reversed.

Despite these changes, Russia and NATO remain the twin poles of nuclear Europe. Pessimistic predictions notwithstanding, nuclear proliferation on the continent has not resumed. Unified Germany has confirmed its renunciation of nuclear weapons. The three former Soviet republics in which nuclear weapons were stationed – Belarus, Kazakstan and Ukraine – have transferred them all to Russia under the 1991 Lisbon Protocol to the Strategic Arms Reduction Talks (START) I Treaty. No other European country is reported to be considering the development of a nuclear arsenal.

NATO now acts as a strategic magnet towards which not only former Warsaw Pact members, but also neutral and non-aligned countries, are increasingly attracted.

Nuclear weapons have left centre-stage in the European defence and security debate. The attention of defence planners and governments now focuses on more salient problems, such as conventional power-projection, peace-support operations or the opportunities of information technologies. However, long-standing NATO nuclear issues persist: the role of British and French nuclear weapons; NATO extended deterrence and the value of the US guarantee; the rationales for the US nuclear presence on the continent; and the impact of missile defences on deterrence in Europe. The future of nuclear weapons in Europe hinges on two broader issues: that of nuclear weapons in general, and that of European security and integration. How will Europe react to the considerable nuclear changes taking place worldwide? Where does the nuclear element fit into Europe's new strategic and political landscape? This paper argues that, despite the end of the Cold War, nuclear weapons remain an important policy instrument in Europe. However, there are challenges and dilemmas ahead which must be managed if the European and transatlantic consensus on nuclear deterrence is to be maintained.

Residual Deterrence in Europe

Europe, NATO and Nuclear Weapons

Despite significant quantitative reductions, on the surface at least the end of the Cold War has not fundamentally altered the European nuclear consensus. No European state challenges either the necessity of maintaining a collective deterrent, or questions European participation and collegiate policy-making.[1] No major political party seems ready to defend the idea of an immediate renunciation of nuclear deterrence.

Although social-democratic and left-leaning political movements tend to be less favourable towards nuclear deterrence than their centre-right or conservative counterparts, attitudes towards nuclear weapons seem to be shaped more by national cultures than by party affiliation. There is a 'core' nuclear Europe, comprising those countries at the historical heart of Western Europe: the Benelux states, France, Germany, Italy and the UK. While not immune to anti-nuclear sensitivities, these states have remained in favour of nuclear deterrence, and are the key players in European nuclear-policy debates. Around this core are four other groups. 'Northern' countries have developed a strategic culture focused on promoting disarmament and peacekeeping, and are deeply interested in the fate of Russia. Neutral or non-aligned states, such as Austria, Ireland and Sweden, often break ranks with the core countries when nuclear issues are tackled in multinational fora such as the UN General Assembly. 'Central/Eastern' countries, mostly former members of the Warsaw Pact, are newcomers to European and Alliance strategic debates, but seem at least willing to consider the advantages of nuclear deterrence. Most Central and Eastern European political leaders have refrained from hostile declarations about nuclear deterrence, and NATO's new members in the region seem to welcome the opportunity to participate in the Alliance's consultative process.[2] Finally, 'Southern' countries generally participate actively in the same nuclear debates, although in Greece and Spain, major anti-nuclear activism associated with perceived US political domination has broken out in the past. These countries are less immediately concerned with Russia, and tend to be more sensitive to proliferation issues given their relative proximity to potential proliferants in North Africa and the Middle East.

Europe's NATO members have diverse positions on nuclear weapons. The UK commits all its forces to the Alliance's integrated military structure. France, while moving closer to this structure in 1996, does not participate in the collective nuclear-planning and consultation process. Belgium, Germany, Greece, Italy, the Netherlands and Turkey are believed to host US nuclear weapons; Denmark and Norway decided in 1957 that they would not do so.[3] Luxembourg, Portugal and Spain have similar policies.

NATO's nuclear solidarity relies on two main collective elements. The first is a set of institutions and procedures. Through the Nuclear Planning Group (NPG), which comprises all NATO members except France (Iceland has observer status), Europeans are briefed by the US and UK on their national postures and policies. They also discuss arms control, proliferation and Russia's nuclear weapons, debate deployment issues, and review Alliance nuclear policy. Meetings are chaired by the NATO Secretary-General, and organised by the NPG Staff Group. A key subordinate body is the High Level Group (HLG), which is chaired by the US. The HLG comprises government experts, and meets several times a year. It is traditionally seen as NATO's internal think-tank for nuclear policy and planning. NATO also organises exercises, seminars and conferences dealing with nuclear-related issues, such as radiation-detection, the safety of nuclear materials and weapons dismantling. NATO Partnership for Peace (PfP) countries are included in some of these activities.

The collective nuclear arsenal permanently stationed in Europe is the second means by which NATO's nuclear solidarity is maintained. These weapons – principally US nuclear gravity bombs for US and European aircraft – are 'an essential and enduring political and military link' between Europe and America.[4] The participation of non-nuclear countries in NATO's nuclear posture 'demonstrates Alliance solidarity, the common commitment of its member countries to maintaining their security, and the widespread sharing among them of burdens and risks'.[5] These weapons also have more implicit functions as vehicles for US influence in Europe, and as safeguards against nuclear proliferation there. Finally, permanently maintaining nuclear weapons in Europe can be justified on the grounds that, should a direct military threat again emerge, it would be easier to augment an existing capacity than to start building one from scratch.[6]

According to most public sources, the US nuclear presence in Europe now amounts to only several hundred gravity bombs, the bulk of which are stationed in Germany, Italy and Turkey (for US and host-country dual-capable aircraft), and in the UK (for American aircraft only). Belgium, Greece and the Netherlands reportedly host a small number of bombs in one air base each solely for use by national aircraft. Legal and budgetary arrangements are contained in bilateral Programs of Cooperation (PoCs). European host nations provide logistic support and other services required by US custodial units.[7] Their air forces are trained, and their aircraft equipped, to deliver US nuclear weapons in wartime under a system requiring a formal US release. NATO nations with no nuclear role would be expected to participate in nuclear missions by 'contributing to the conventional support packages (sweep, escort, defence suppression, electronic warfare, tanker, AWACS [airborne warning and control system] etc.) that would be needed to allow [dual-capable aircraft] to penetrate their target(s)'.[8] In 1995, the NPG 'provided guidance to adapt force posture to the current security environment'; the following year, it reported that 'the readiness of NATO's dual-capable aircraft has ... been adapted'.[9] Some analysts suggest that only one unit per country is now maintained at high readiness.[10]

European officers, mostly British and German, are assigned to NATO nuclear staff in the small International Staff's Nuclear Policy Directorate, and in the International Military Staff's NBC Policy Branch. They are also assigned to the Supreme Headquarters Allied

Powers Europe (SHAPE) Special Weapons Branch, which is responsible for conducting NATO's collective nuclear planning. During the Cold War, there was a European presence at the now-disbanded US Strategic Air Command (SAC) in Omaha, Nebraska, where 'deconfliction' (eliminating redundancies, for example) between NATO and US strategic targeting was achieved. Americans still hold the key positions in both the military and civilian sides of the Alliance's nuclear machinery. The US nuclear role in NATO and the country's general influence in the Alliance military-command structure remain closely linked to one another. The fact that the Supreme Allied Commander Europe (SACEUR) is of American nationality is believed to be at the heart of the transatlantic security contract.

In 1990, NATO's London Summit communiqué referred to nuclear systems as 'weapons of last resort'.[11] However, the following year, while preparing the Strategic Concept to be adopted at NATO's Rome Summit, President George Bush's administration quietly dropped this expression because it could imply a downgrading of nuclear deterrence, with which France and the UK were uncomfortable. The Strategic Concept issued in Rome was vague, essentially making nuclear weapons a decisive, but hidden, advantage. Under the Concept, nuclear arms make 'a unique contribution in rendering the risks of any aggression incalculable and unacceptable', even though the circumstances in which their use might have to be contemplated by NATO have become 'even more remote'.[12] On 21–22 October 1992, the NPG adopted new principles for consultations and nuclear planning. According to a German White Paper in 1994, NATO's nuclear planning 'is not directed towards a tangible threat'.[13] In 1996, the Allies declared that their nuclear forces 'are not targeted against anyone', thereby abandoning pre-planning for sub-strategic use.[14]

nuclear forces have no formal targets

No public collective statement has complemented this purposely minimalist doctrinal corpus. However, statements by British officials hint at the existence of two concepts: strategic use; and sub- or non-strategic use, which would be a 'political message of the Alliance's resolve to defend itself'.[15] As described by a British official:

> *a substrategic strike would be the limited and highly*
> *selective use of nuclear weapons in a manner that fell*
> *demonstrably short of a strategic strike, but with a sufficient*
> *level of violence to convince an aggressor who had already*
> *miscalculated our resolve and attacked us that he should halt*
> *his aggression and withdraw or face the prospect of a*
> *devastating strategic strike.*[16]

In 1997, the Allies made a political commitment to Russia not to undertake any major modifications to their strategy and, in the NATO–Russia Founding Act of 1997, reiterated that they saw no 'need to change any aspect of NATO's nuclear posture or nuclear policy'.[17] In the run-up to the Washington Summit in April 1999, the Alliance's three nuclear powers agreed that it was not necessary to change the Strategic Concept's language on nuclear weapons, a view shared by most of NATO's non-nuclear members.

French and British National Strategies
France
France's deterrent arsenal was significantly reduced following President Jacques Chirac's 1995–96 defence review. *Hadès* land-based short-range ballistic missiles (SRBMs), S-3D land-based inter-mediate-range ballistic missiles (IRBMs) and *Mirage* IVP bombers were retired in 1996. Under the '2015 Model' defined by the defence review, the French nuclear-deterrent posture has been significantly trimmed, and is now based on a dyad.[18] Its sea-based element comprises four ballistic-missile submarines (SSBNs), with one or two on patrol at all times. *Redoutable*-class submarines are being replaced by new-generation *Triomphant*-class SSBNs. The first – the *Triomphant* itself – was admitted to active duty in March 1997. Three others are to follow, the *Téméraire* in 1999 and the *Vigilant* in 2003; a fourth should enter service in 2008. These SSBNs are able to carry the new M45 missile with up to six multiple independently targetable re-entry vehicle (MIRV) warheads each. From 2008, the M45 will be replaced by a new missile, the M51, with an increased range and a different set of nuclear warheads. Due to the end of testing, this will not be a 'new type', but a more 'robust' version of existing designs.

A nuclear air component complements these SSBNs, consisting of a *Mirage* 2000N fleet of about 45 dual-capable aircraft in three squadrons, and of modernised carrier-based *Super Etendards*. These aircraft, which carry the *Air-Sol, Moyenne Portée* (ASMP) ramjet-propelled supersonic missile, are to be gradually replaced at the turn of the century by the *Rafale*. At the end of its service life, the ASMP will be replaced by an 'Enhanced ASMP' of the same family, but incorporating technological improvements and performance gains, particularly increased range and better penetration capacities. It is assumed that, in its Navy version, the *Rafale*, which will be based on the aircraft carrier *Charles de Gaulle*, could also carry the Enhanced ASMP. France is now the only Western nuclear power to maintain a carrier-based nuclear capacity and, since Russia is supposed to have withdrawn all of its 'tactical' sea-based nuclear weapons, may be the only nuclear country in the world to do so.

Warhead and missile numbers have not been publicly announced, save for the fact that the SSBN force would have only three sets of warheads because one submarine will always be in dry dock. It is generally assumed that France's arsenal is larger than the UK's given the country's full independence from the US and NATO weapons. In French eyes, the UK can afford a lighter, more relaxed operational posture because its nuclear weapons would normally be 'backed' by those of the US and NATO.

As during the Cold War, French nuclear weapons still protect the country's 'vital interests' as defined by the president, and the yardstick by which sufficiency is measured remains the capacity to inflict unacceptable damage on an adversary. However, a White Paper in 1994 opened three new avenues for French nuclear strategy. According to the Paper, 'the credibility of [the French] deterrent posture relies on the availability of facilities that are sufficiently flexible and diversified to offer the Head of State a variety of options when required'.[19] By introducing the words 'flexible' and 'diversified' into nuclear doctrine, the White Paper seemed to acknowledge that deterrence could include a more subtle approach than that reflected in the full-blown counter-cities strike planned against the Soviet Union. Second, the Paper raised the possibility of moving towards a European deterrent, the first official government document ever to do so: 'with [a] nuclear potential, Europe's autonomy with regard to defence is possible. Without it, it is not'.[20]

Finally, the White Paper identified two typical cases where nuclear deterrence could play a role: the classic major-threat scenario, called S6 ('Resurgence of a major threat against Western Europe'), and also a more innovative S2 situation entitled 'Regional conflict that may involve our vital interests'. By expanding deterrence to include regional states, France was acknowledging that its vital interests could be threatened by a country other than a major power. Since the White Paper, a number of French presidential and government statements have made clear that deterrence also encompassed chemical and biological weapons if the country's vital interests were at stake.

Coincident with the White Paper, France decided to participate in the NATO Senior Defence Group on Proliferation (DGP), set up by the Alliance Summit in January 1994. In its capacity as DGP co-chair, France played a particularly important role in drafting the common risk assessment which was the object of the first phase of NATO's work. French involvement in the DGP is indicative of the country's new-found willingness to play a key role in non-proliferation. France has actively promoted the Nuclear Non-Proliferation Treaty (NPT)'s renewal, the Comprehensive Test Ban Treaty (CTBT) and a fissile material cut-off regime.

While the broad consensus on nuclear deterrence is intact (even the Communists and Greens have taken relatively moderate positions), issues such as testing and NATO policy have prompted political debate. Few French experts have called for rapid nuclear disarmament, and the main topic of discussion is not whether a nuclear *debate over nuclear use* deterrent should be maintained, but *in regional conflict* whether it should or could play a role *vis-à-vis* regional adversaries armed with weapons of mass destruction (WMD). Major policy changes are unlikely in the short term. Most Socialist experts, as well as officials like Foreign Minister Hubert Védrine, are generally conservative on nuclear issues.[21] In his first major defence-policy speech in September 1997, Socialist Prime Minister Lionel Jospin reaffirmed the bases of his country's nuclear policy, emphasising its importance to 'preserve [France's] freedom of action', and stating that France would 'continue its strategic reflection in order to adapt continuously its doctrine and means to the evolution of potential threats'.[22]

Table 1 *European Nuclear Forces*

1999	
France	
2 *Redoutable*-class SSBNs	16 M4 SLBMs (96 warheads) per SSBN
2 *Triomphant*-class SSBNs	16 M45 SLBMs per SSBN
Mirage 2000N	1 ASMP missile per aircraft
Super Etendard	1 ASMP missile per aircraft
UK	
3 *Vanguard*-class SSBNs	16 *Trident* 2D5 SLBMs (48 warheads) per SSBN
2009	
France	
3 *Triomphant*-class SSBNs	16 M45 SLBMs per SSBN
1 *Triomphant*-class SSBN	16 M51 SLBMs per SSBN
Rafale-Air	1 ASMP-A missile per aircraft
Rafale-Marine	1 ASMP-A missile per aircraft
UK	
4 *Vanguard*-class SSBNs	16 *Trident* 2D5 SLBMs per SSBN

The UK

The UK also has substantially reduced its nuclear arsenal. Following the disbanding of its air-based nuclear capability on 31 March 1998 and the removal of its decades-old nuclear presence in mainland Europe, the country is now the world's first nuclear state to rely exclusively on a submarine force.[23] This comprises *Trident* missiles and *Vanguard*-class submarines, which are replacing first-generation SSBNs. HMS *Vanguard* became operational in December 1994, HMS *Victorious* in January 1996 and HMS *Vigilant* in 1998. The fourth, HMS *Vengeance*, should enter service by 2000. Only one submarine will be on strategic patrol at all times, while another will be ready to be loaded with both strategic and sub-strategic missiles.[24]

Besides being cheaper than a new airborne missile for sub-strategic missions, *Trident* was apparently judged to offer other advantages – in particular, a higher probability of fulfilling such missions due to its reliability and penetration capacity, and its freedom from basing, over-flight and refuelling problems. According to British officials, *Trident* offers three-fold flexibility: in the choice of targets; in the number of warheads per missile; and in warhead yield.[25] Compared to the *Polaris* system which it replaces, *Trident* has improved range and precision, a higher load capacity per missile, and MIRV technology allowing separate warhead targeting.

In 1993, the government announced that the *Vanguard* SSBNs would carry no more than 96 warheads, although it was later made known that the routine load was 60 per submarine, significantly lower than the 128-warhead ceiling envisaged by Prime Minister Margaret Thatcher's government.[26] In 1996, it was announced that the UK's arsenal included 'less than 300 operationally available' warheads and, the following year, that 65 *Trident* missiles were to be bought from the US.[27] The Strategic Defence Review (SDR) completed by Prime Minister Tony Blair's Labour government in 1998 reduced these numbers to 'less than 200 operationally available' (48 per SSBN), and only 58 missiles were to be bought from the US. The SDR fulfilled the pledge made by the Labour Party when in opposition in 1996 that the *Trident* system would not deploy more warheads than had *Polaris*, but did so in such a way that it arguably fell short of Labour's 'freeze'.[28] The SDR confirmed that *Polaris* was originally deployed with three warheads per missile (48 per SSBN), and later with only two (32 per submarine). Thus, the government's claim that 48 warheads per SSBN under *Trident* did not exceed the *Polaris* deployment was correct only in terms of the original *Trident* complement. Since it is unlikely that the UK's four SSBNs could all put to sea at the same time, the country's 200 operational warheads, plus some 'non-operationally available' ones kept in reserve, mean that it has sufficient surplus capacity to be able to increase the number of warheads per submarine if necessary.

British officials are keen to emphasise that the UK's missiles are 'operationally entirely independent of the US and do not require any US data or inputs in order to be targeted and fired'.[29] British nuclear doctrine is, however, largely symbiotic with that of the US, and with NATO's collective doctrine. As the second nuclear power in the Alliance's integrated structure, the UK has a key input into NATO nuclear policies, and continues to play a central role in its collective deterrent. On taking office in May 1997, the Labour government immediately confirmed that it 'fully supports NATO policy on the continuing requirement for a substrategic capability as a crucial element of credible deterrence'.[30] The UK's posture makes clear that deterring a major threat remains the fundamental rationale for its nuclear arsenal, and *Trident*'s possible utility in deterring WMD use by regional adversaries has been given little publicity.[31]

Post-Cold War nuclear debates in the two European nuclear countries do not exactly mirror each other. The debate in the UK concerns the continued relevance of the country's deterrent as a whole, whereas the French debate concerns more the question of deterrence *vis-à-vis* new risks. This follows a historical pattern, in which the principle of nuclear deterrence is traditionally discussed in the UK, while only its scope and details tend to be debated in France. However, the UK and France share the same perspective on the NPT, the CTBT, a fissile material cut-off regime, NSAs and nuclear-weapon-free zones. They also concur on the interpretation of the International Court of Justice (ICJ)'s 1996 advisory opinion, which failed to condemn the possession of nuclear weapons or, in extreme circumstances, their use. The Labour Party's manifesto pledges included a treaty on NSAs and a negotiated, multilateral no-first-use agreement between the nuclear powers. By early 1999, Blair's government had yet to demonstrate its willingness to implement these ideas.

The Nuclear Status Quo

Since the end of the Cold War, European strategic debates have focused on modernising and reorganising conventional forces. In the absence of a major threat, there is no obvious need to discuss nuclear deterrence, either its 'software' (doctrines and declaratory policies), or its 'hardware' (systems and operations). The dramatic decline in NATO's collective nuclear capacity means that there are fewer technical and operational issues to discuss. Nuclear bases, installations and staff have been cut considerably since 1989, and a 'consolidation' process begun in 1992–93 has reduced permanent

US storage sites.[32] Since post-Cold War nuclear options would likelihood involve fewer weapons than in the past, most Europ countries would probably not participate in nuclear missio. themselves, lessening the need to debate risks and responsibilities.

Within NATO, fewer meetings are devoted to nuclear-policy issues. The NPG now convenes only at ministerial level and generally with a short agenda. Most meetings last hours, instead of one or two days, as they did during the Cold War. Nuclear exercises and war-gaming have been reduced to a minimum. National defence doctrines barely mention nuclear deterrence, let alone nuclear participation or Alliance doctrine. Fewer European military officers and civil servants are assigned to Alliance nuclear staff, either at military or political level, and fewer experts deal with nuclear issues in national bureaucracies. Thus, fewer of them are sensitive to nuclear issues, or trained to deal with them. This leads to misperceptions, even in well-informed circles. In a report to the US Congress in 1996, for instance, prominent expert Stanley Sloan described possible 'incompatibilities between NATO's official description of nuclear systems as weapons of "last resort" and French support for nuclear warning shots against an advancing enemy', thereby effectively misconstruing both Allied and French doctrines.[33]

The presence of US nuclear bombs in Europe now goes virtually unnoticed, to the point where some experts and journalists assert that they have all been withdrawn. A 1996 report for the European Parliament, for example, made this claim without prompting any official denial, while in the same year the British media reported that

US nuclear weapons go virtually unnoticed

all US nuclear weapons had been removed from UK territory.[34] In 1997, Giuseppe Cucchi, then an advisor to the Italian government, wrote that it was credible to think that there were no US nuclear weapons left in Europe.[35] Neither NATO nor its individual governments appears keen to resolve this ambiguity. Apart from the UK and Germany, where the 1994 White Paper explicitly mentions German nuclear participation and the stationing of US weapons on German soil, NATO governments are deliberately vague.[36] When the environmental organisation Greenpeace published a list of supposed US nuclear deployments in 1995, the Belgian Air Force acknowledged such a presence, but the Greek government refused to confirm or deny that US nuclear weapons were on its soil.[37]

Deterrence in Europe seems increasingly to be comprised of two components. The first, including the bulk of forces in terms of numbers and explosive power, is made up of submarine-launched ballistic missiles. It remains largely national, and acts as a deterrent against a major threat. The second component comprises nuclear air forces, which complement the first, and allow selective strikes in order to deter more limited threats. American, British and French policies are leading to a simplified, residual and less visible nuclear deterrent, based on a silent or 'default' consensus. The following chapter describes the unfolding challenges to this nuclear status quo.

chapter 2

Challenges to Europe's Nuclear Status Quo

Since the early 1990s, both the scope and the means of nuclear deterrence have been restricted, and the number of countries giving up procuring a national nuclear arsenal, or removing nuclear weapons from their territory, has increased. Nuclear arsenals have been steadily reduced, and the development of nuclear warheads has been constrained by the CTBT and self-imposed fissile-material-production cut-offs. Non-aligned countries and non-governmental organisations (NGOs) are increasingly voicing their opposition to the continued possession of nuclear weapons. As a result of these changes, claims that nuclear deterrence is in danger of being 'delegitimised' have become commonplace.

While these developments are meaningful, the importance of this trend seems overrated, and its novelty arguable. Delegit-imisation has been a key term in the Western strategic debate since the 1980s. As far back as the 1970s, Alliance countries had effectively ceased to consider nuclear weapons as war-fighting tools. Delegit-imisation was boosted in the 1980s with the Reagan administration's promotion of the Strategic Defense Initiative (SDI). The complete elimination of nuclear weapons was considered at the US–Soviet Summit in Reykjavik in 1986. The world's first nuclear-disarmament agreement, the Intermediate-range Nuclear Forces (INF) Treaty, was signed in 1987. Anti-nuclear resolutions were regularly adopted by the UN General Assembly during the Cold War. Indeed, nuclear debates today make less impact on public opinion than they did at peak periods of East–West tension, when demonstrations in Bonn, Brussels, London or Madrid attracted hundreds of thousands of people.[1]

There are, in fact, good reasons to believe that nuclear weapons will be with us for some time to come. The NPT has been renewed indefinitely. The ICJ's advisory opinion failed to condemn the possession of nuclear weapons or, in extreme circumstances, their use. Implementing a START III Treaty would only cut the number of accountable strategic weapons to 1960s' levels – when there was already talk of 'overkill'. The concept of nuclear deterrence has survived the end of the Cold War. In large parts of the world, nuclear weapons seem to have more, rather than less, legitimacy. Both India and Pakistan have shown themselves willing to challenge the international nuclear order, while Russia and China increasingly view nuclear weapons as key elements of their military power and international status. Half the world's people and land surface remains under a 'nuclear shadow'.

the concept of nuclear deterrence has survived

Nonetheless, the deterrence status quo in Europe faces many challenges. The consensus on deterrence is not as solid as it may appear at first sight; rather, it is volatile and becoming increasingly difficult to maintain. US attitudes towards nuclear weapons, including in an Alliance context, are changing. The Euro-Atlantic political and security architecture is evolving, modifying the way in which links between nuclear powers are organised. Finally, the growing strategic importance of WMD proliferation has prompted a new debate in Europe over the possible role of nuclear weapons in deterring this threat.

The Eroding Elite Consensus

During the Cold War, large segments of Western public opinion actively favoured removing US nuclear weapons from Europe, and mobilised to press their case.[2] But Europe's political élites, conservative and social-democrat alike, generally stood firm and, even at the height of East–West tension, the nuclear consensus within the Alliance was preserved. With the end of the Cold War, however, the reverse seems to be true. While public opinion has adopted an the overwhelming conventional military threat posed by the old Soviet bloc'.[21]

The Changing Euro-Atlantic Political Architecture

The third challenge to the Cold War consensus on deterrence stems from changes in the framework of Euro-Atlantic political and security relations. In some respects, this architecture has remained surprisingly intact. Far from disappearing or being replaced, either by the Organisation for Security and Cooperation in Europe (OSCE) or the WEU, NATO more than ever is at the centre of Europe's security structure. Alliance credibility has been reinforced by the new relations developed with NATO's former Warsaw Pact enemies, by its engagement in the Yugoslav crisis and by other significant adaptations such as its work on WMD proliferation.

Nonetheless, qualitative changes have taken place. As the shadow of the Bosnian crisis dissipated, institutions became able to embark on a second phase of adaptation after the initial adjustments made at the start of the 1990s. In May 1997, the NATO–Russia Founding Act, designed to pave the way for a new, cooperative relationship between the continent's two major security poles, was signed. At the European Union (EU)'s Amsterdam Summit the following month, member-states confirmed the Economic and Monetary Union (EMU) process, agreed to reinforce the EU's role in security and defence issues, strengthened its links with the WEU and opened the door to further EU enlargement. In July, NATO heads of state and government agreed to begin talks on admitting the Czech Republic, Hungary and Poland, strengthened the European identity within Alliance military structures and decided to revise NATO's Strategic Concept. Concrete development of a European security and defence identity, endorsed at NATO's 1996 Berlin Ministerial Meeting, was boosted in 1998 by the Anglo-French Declaration of Saint Malo. The Declaration stated that 'the EU needs to be in a position to play its full role on the international scene', and that 'to this end, [it] must have the capacity for autonomous action, backed up by credible military forces'.[22] The birth of the European single currency in 1999, and the adoption of NATO's new Strategic Concept at the Washington Summit, appeared set to close this transition phase.

The growing interdependence of Western defence strategies is also important. For both political reasons (multinational forces being a symbol of solidarity) and budgetary purposes, a large number of combined forces have been created, either in a NATO or in an *ad hoc* European context, since 1991. This has had an indirect impact on deterrence policies. As the coordination of security strategies and military forces grows, political interests tend to become increasingly shared.

Finally, the enlargement of European institutions means that countries lacking the 'nuclear education' of the Cold War now participate directly in the European strategic debate. Finland, Ireland and Sweden refused to subscribe to the paragraph dealing with nuclear deterrence in the text on European security interests adopted by the WEU in Madrid in November 1995. In contrast with the situation prevailing during the Cold War, only a minority of EU states have nuclear weapons stationed on their territory. As a result, a strategic culture which includes nuclear deterrence at its core will be increasingly less evident in the political debates taking place in European fora.

These developments will affect the future of nuclear deterrence in Europe in two main ways. As new countries join NATO, questions arise over whether they should be covered by the same nuclear 'umbrella' enjoyed by older members, while the evolving relationship with Moscow raises doubts over whether it is desirable and feasible to maintain some form of deterrence in relation to Russia. Second, as European integration proceeds, should it assume a nuclear dimension? Could this coexist with an unchanged NATO deterrent?

Evolving Nuclear Relationships

Nuclear relationships within NATO are also changing. During the Cold War, nuclear solidarity within the Alliance revolved largely around a double axis: a US–British one inherited from the Second World War, with close cooperation on nuclear technologies, systems and planning; and an Anglo-German one, based on political cooperation within NATO's NPG, including policy elaboration, and on the presence of Royal Air Force (RAF) bases in Germany.[23] Following the end of the Cold War, this pattern seems to be changing. Anglo-American nuclear convergence is weakening, while a strong partnership is developing between London and Paris.[24] Although this relationship has not developed from scratch, it is nonetheless one of the most remarkable features of the European nuclear scene. Anglo-French exchanges and cooperation projects have taken place since the 1970s; a plan to build a joint nuclear-capable long-range missile, for example, was developed in the late 1980s.[25] But the relationship was given fresh impetus in 1992, when then British Secretary of State for Defence Malcolm Rifkind and his French counterpart Pierre Joxe agreed to create a Joint Commission on Nuclear Policy and Doctrine. The Commission comprises a small number of senior officials from the policy departments of the British and French defence and foreign ministries. Members of the two countries' defence staffs and other officials also occasionally participate.

The Commission presented its first Report to Ministers – a substantive paper covering issues such as nuclear doctrines, NSAs, the European dimension of deterrence, anti-missile defences, disarmament and nuclear testing – at the July 1993 Franco-British Summit. At the Summit, then President François Mitterrand and Prime Minister John Major agreed to make the Joint Commission a permanent body, stating that it had established 'a number of [common] concepts in the field of nuclear deterrence, of nuclear arms control, and nonproliferation'.[26] According to Rifkind, the Commission

new Anglo-French nuclear cooperation

testified to the fact that there was 'no difference between France and the United Kingdom on the fundamental nuclear issues'.[27] The intimacy and secrecy of the Joint Commission's work helped to create an atmosphere promoting frankness and understanding; joint position papers, even on the most sensitive subjects, were produced with relative ease.

After the UK's decision not to pursue the joint long-range missile programme in 1993, the Commission gained in prominence as a way to deepen nuclear discussions between London and Paris. The concept of deterrence in relation to 'new risks' – that is, threats other than massive aggression in Europe – was discussed. A milestone was reached in 1995 when Major and new President Jacques Chirac announced that they '[did] not see situations arising in which the vital interests of either France or the United Kingdom could be threatened without the vital interests of the other also being threatened'. The pair also decided to 'pursue and deepen nuclear cooperation', aiming 'mutually to strengthen deterrence, while retaining the independence' of both countries' nuclear forces, and noted that deepening Anglo-French cooperation would 'strengthen the European contribution to overall deterrence'.[28] The recognition of common vital interests means that the joint exercise of nuclear deterrence has become theoretically possible. Given the shared interests at stake, the idea that one country could act on the other's behalf should their political leaders so decide is no longer far-fetched. The nuclear relationship between France and the UK has been radically transformed.

The strong French drive for European defence integration, increasing cooperation with the UK and *rapprochement* with NATO since 1993 make it possible to argue that there are no longer any strictly national nuclear deterrents in Europe. Since the end of the Cold War, all the Allies, France included, have worked together on most key issues with a nuclear dimension: elaborating the Strategic Concept, in which France played a key role, and subsequently revising it in 1999; WMD proliferation; the implications of enlargement; and the activities of the NATO–Russia Permanent Joint Council (PJC).[29]

Finally, the relative share of European nuclear forces on the continent has grown dramatically, from some 10% of permanently stationed US forces in the 1970s and 1980s to roughly equivalent numbers (several hundred weapons, according to most public sources) by the end of the 1990s. Europe's nuclear weight is thus now much greater, in relative terms, than it was during the Cold War. British and French nuclear weapons are no longer in the shadow of a colossal US nuclear presence.

WMD Proliferation

The fourth challenge to nuclear deterrence in Europe stems from the growing strategic importance of WMD proliferation. The direct WMD threat to European territory is at present limited or non-existent. However, post-Cold War developments, such as the reported cooperation between China and North Korea and various Middle Eastern and Mediterranean Basin countries on ballistic missiles and technologies, are of growing European concern. At least

20 states are reported to have a chemical and/or biological-weapons programme for military purposes. While the number of countries armed with nuclear weapons is likely to remain limited, Iraq and North Korea show how difficult it is to curb a nuclear-weapons programme undertaken by motivated leaders. WMD are attractive because they are seen, rightly or wrongly, as cost-effective strategic tools, either as weapons or as instruments of political power. In particular, they have come to be perceived as equalising, politically or militarily, a powerful conventional adversary or coalition.

Broadly, European countries could be directly affected by a WMD threat in two situations. An adversary could use WMD in an attempt to disrupt coalition military operations in a theatre, or could attempt to blackmail intervening countries or their allies by threatening to use WMD-armed missiles against their cities. The possible role of nuclear weapons in deterring threats such as these has become a new subject of debate in Europe.

The Indian and Pakistani nuclear tests in 1998 revealed supplementary challenges. Europe cannot remain immune to the emergence of two new nuclear powers, particularly since France and the UK are 'official' nuclear-weapon states and Permanent Members of the UN Security Council. While the UN, the Group of Eight (G-8) industrial nations and the US, rather than Europe, have been at the forefront of efforts to manage the consequences of these tests, many believe that a dialogue between European countries and India and Pakistan would be both legitimate and useful. The tests have also highlighted the fragility of the link between nuclear weapons and permanent membership of the Security Council. The idea that non-nuclear countries such as Germany or Japan deserve a permanent seat is already widespread. If the suggestion that India should give up its nuclear weapons in order to gain a similar privilege gained support, the link would be strained further. Although this is a longer-term issue, it could affect thinking in France and the UK, both about their position, and that of Europe as a whole, in the world.

chapter 3

Adapting Nuclear Strategies in Europe

The primary purpose of nuclear weapons is to enhance security. Since the end of the Cold War, several strategic rationales for their continued presence in Europe have been put forward: they contribute to making major war unthinkable; they help to prevent the possible use of WMD against European interests; and they limit conventional arms races. Nuclear weapons may also help in moderating possible future tensions between Russia and its former Warsaw Pact neighbours and, perhaps, assist in discouraging Russia from using nuclear weapons in conflicts outside Europe.

However, trying to develop a cooperative relationship with Russia based on trust, while at the same time ensuring a continued deterrent against Moscow, including for new NATO members, will increasingly border on strategic schizophrenia. Likewise, it will be difficult to emphasise the role of nuclear weapons in deterrence, while playing down their importance for non-proliferation purposes. These are the complexities of the emerging European debates on adapting nuclear strategies, which include nuclear doctrines, NATO's collective deterrent and arms control and disarmament.

Debating Nuclear Doctrines
Deterring Major Threats

Due to Europe's geographic location, most Europeans remain preoccupied by the possibility of a 'major' threat, that is, a threat from a large power on the Eurasian landmass. No one in Europe believes that a major conventional threat on the continent could emerge in the near future, but there is nonetheless reluctance to abandon the military and doctrinal apparatus that might be needed in the distant future, and that has political utility in the present. As Rifkind put it in 1992, NATO strategy 'makes military recidivism by any future Russian leadership a pointless option for them'.[1] Hence, many Europeans are unwilling to embrace a no-first-use pledge, even in the absence of a major classical threat, and are sceptical about 'conventional deterrence'.

In addition, many remain concerned about the possibility, in the medium term, of a more limited or regional conflict involving Russia, which now shares a long border with the EU. Ensuring the security of geographically vulnerable countries such as Poland or the Baltic states will become increasingly recognised as a major policy objective for the Allies. Russia's still vast arsenal of tactical/theatre nuclear weapons – put at between 7,000 and 12,000 – is thus a cause for concern, particularly in Germany.[2] In 1995, Christian Democratic Union (CDU) disarmament spokesman Friedbert Pflüger claimed that no one could convince him that 'in five, or maybe two or three years, some dictator won't rule the Kremlin who is holding 25,000 nuclear weapons'.[3]

Russia still poses an 'existential' nuclear threat

In Poland, the question of Russian weapons in the Kaliningrad enclave is a worry. In Turkey, concerns have been raised about the perceived expansion of the Russian nuclear umbrella since 1993 as former-Soviet republics such as Georgia have signed military treaties with Moscow.[4] The residual deterrence function of nuclear weapons *vis-à-vis* an 'existential' Russian nuclear threat tends to be seen as their main purpose by Eastern European leaders. In 1997, Czech President Vaclav Havel stated that nuclear weapons serve as a deterrent only where there is a 'big strategic enemy'.[5]

Could nations other than Russia pose a major threat to Europe? China's intercontinental ballistic missiles (ICBMs) could reach European territory but, unlike in the US, predictions of direct conflict with China do not have much credibility in Europe, and are rarely discussed. Nonetheless, there are situations in which China could pose a potential threat. Beijing could seek to neutralise European interference in an Asian crisis – for example, in support of a US military intervention to protect South Korea, Taiwan or Japan – or could attempt to blackmail the US by threatening to target its European allies. China could attempt to oppose a European military intervention against a regional ally trying to seize control of Gulf oil reserves or other resources. Europe could feel compelled to side with Russia should a Sino-Russian conflict break out in the distant future. While at present none of these hypothetical situations has made China's nuclear weapons salient for Europeans, this could change in the future.

What kind of targets should be selected to deter major threats in the future? In the absence of a specific, immediate threat, targeting is less central for 'day-to-day' deterrence than it was in the past. It seems clear that, with the end of the Cold War, targeting is likely to allow increased flexibility in deterrence. Command, control and communications and computer technologies have improved to the point where nuclear plans tailored to a crisis can be devised almost in 'real time', to ensure that deterrence is credible against a specific threat. This will help in coping with the diversity of possible future risks, since post-Cold War 'non-global' threats would perhaps not be deterred by the prospect of massive retaliation entailing considerable destruction. In addition, developments in international law strengthening legal norms governing armed warfare may prompt policy-makers to ensure that their deterrence plans include options that, for instance, do not target populations as such. Since nuclear weapons are not war-fighting arms, the importance of such self-imposed constraints is debatable. But deterrence also relies on the perception that the possessor of nuclear weapons is confident of their political efficiency, and would not hesitate to use them if necessary. Since increased flexibility and diversity in targeting will help to ensure that political leaders are confident in the value of their country's nuclear deterrent, deterrence may be reinforced.

Nuclear Deterrence and WMD

While many of those countries suspected of pursuing active nuclear, biological and chemical (NBC) research and development programmes are in Europe's vicinity (in North Africa or the Middle East), the European debate over whether nuclear weapons can deter WMD use by regional powers has not developed as far as it has in the US. Both France and the UK have excluded any war-fighting role

nuclear weapons in a regional conflict, but recognise that nuclear
errence can have a function outside of the East–West context, and
ve probably given more consideration to this issue than most of
their European allies. Nonetheless, the precise scope of the interests
that would be covered by nuclear deterrence in regional contin-
gencies remains uncertain. National territories are undoubtedly
considered 'vital' interests, but it is unclear whether a WMD strike
on, for example, an expeditionary unit would elicit a nuclear
response. Both Paris and London are deliberately ambiguous on this
issue, although neither wants to rely solely on nuclear deterrence to
protect its forces, and both acknowledge the need for 'extended air
defences', perhaps including theatre missile defences.

The French declaratory policy concerning WMD deterrence is
complex. In 1992, Chirac expressed the view that nuclear deterrence
was valid where biological and conventional weapons were
concerned.[6] As president, he confirmed his belief that WMD could
threaten vital interests: 'Only the [nuclear] deterrent force guarantees
France against the possible use of weapons of mass destruction, of
whatever type they may be'.[7] In the run-up to the NPT Review and
Extension Conference in 1995, Paris not only agreed to harmonise its
NSAs with those of the other nuclear powers, but also, for the first
time, issued positive security assurances (PSAs). To ensure that its
NSAs, while benefiting global non-proliferation efforts, did not
constrain France's ability to protect its vital interests, Paris set
specific conditions under which they would apply.[8] First, they were
reserved only for those NPT members which were 'respecting' their
commitments; second, France retained the 'right to self defence in
accordance with Article 51 of the
United Nations Charter'; and third,
the French deterrent would continue
to cover 'any threat against our vital
interests, and this is valid whatever the means and the origins of the
threats, including of course that of weapons of mass destruction'.[9]
These statements constituted a particular interpretation of the
meaning and limitations of the country's NSAs by creating two
caveats to them. First, an adversary using chemical or biological
weapons against French vital interests would be exposed to what, in
legal terms, is known as a 'belligerent reprisal', where violating a
legal norm (in this case, the NSA) can be justified if the adversary

*the argument for nuclear
deterrence of WMD threats*

has first violated another (either the NPT or the Biological and Chemical Weapons Conventions). Second, the principle of self-defence embodied in Article 51 was an inalienable right. Policies since 1995 have remained faithful to this line. In 1997, Jospin mentioned proliferation as one rationale for France to keep nuclear weapons.[10]

The UK's position is similar. Due to its geographic location, British territory would be less vulnerable to a medium-range missile threat than that of its southern neighbours. However, the global role which the UK wants to play, its responsibilities within NATO and the possibility that proliferants could increase the range of their missiles mean that the country has an interest in deterring WMD. The British language tends to be more implicit than the French. Lawrence Freedman's phrasing is typical:

> It is hard to see how Western countries can make explicit nuclear threats to deter chemical or biological use. Apart from legal obligations not to use nuclear weapons against non-nuclear states, it would be difficult to make retaliation automatic, given that such an attack might turn out to be poorly targeted and to have limited results. Nonetheless, at the same time it would be unwise for any would-be perpetrator to assume that an attack which caused immense suffering and a vast loss of life would not generate such anger that nuclear use would become a real possibility.[11]

Then Defence Minister Rifkind stated in September 1992 that 'considerable' questions were raised concerning deterrence in relation to a regional aggressor, in particular its understanding of deterrence policies. It was thus probably reasonable to assume that regional deterrence would only be useful in the case of a 'direct threat to national homelands'.[12] The following year, however, he warned that the UK's NSAs should not be interpreted as a 'green light' for chemical or biological aggression, and emphasised that 'the context in which we extend [NSAs] is one in which we attach ever increasing importance to the Biological Weapons and Chemical Weapons Conventions'.[13] This could imply that a regional power using such weapons would in a sense 'outlaw' itself, and thus be exposed to a nuclear strike despite the NSAs – a concept close to that put forward by the French. Finally, Rifkind stressed that suggesting a potential role for nuclear weapons outside the East–West context should not be interpreted as a move towards giving them a war-fighting function.[14]

British officials have since confirmed the potential role of nuclear weapons to deter WMD aggression.[15] The 1998 SDR restated the relevance of a potential regional role for deterrence, albeit indirectly: in a regional conflict involving NATO, it was necessary, according to the SDR, to maintain 'a capability to deter the threat or use of nuclear weapons'.[16] Armed Forces Minister John Reid confirmed the continuity of UK thinking when he stated in 1998 that 'it seems unlikely that a dictator who was willing to strike another country with WMDs would be so trusting as to feel entirely sure that that country would not respond with the power at its disposal'.[17] In terms of the specific threat of a chemical or biological strike, the language used by the UK to describe its response is carefully crafted and deliberately vague because of the issue's legal and political sensitivity: 'the use of chemical or biological weapons by any State would be a grave breach of international law. A State which chose to use chemical or biological weapons against the UK should expect us to exercise our right of self-defence and to make a proportionate response'.[18]

Alliance efforts to adapt policies and strategies to face such threats have helped to develop European-wide thinking in this area, notably through the work of the Senior Political–Military Group on Proliferation (SGP) and the DGP, which is co-chaired by the US and a European country. The HLG has also tackled these issues. Some basic NATO doctrinal principles on the role of nuclear weapons in relation to new risks have been established. As described by Alliance officials, these seem to involve a mix of deterrence through the threat of 'punishment' and through the threat of 'denial', which implies that hostile WMD arsenals could be targeted if deterrence failed.[19] According to a European NATO official, 'we have recognized that the nuclear posture of the Alliance could play a helpful part in deterring rogue states from using weapons of mass destruction'.[20] A NATO fact sheet issued in November 1997 confirmed that 'together with an appropriate mix of conventional capability, [NATO's nuclear forces] also create uncertainty for any country that might contemplate seeking political or military advantage through the threat or use of weapons of mass destruction against the Alliance'.[21] Agreement on the utility of nuclear weapons in deterring WMD is stronger in those countries most heavily involved in the fora discussing these issues (the UK, Germany and the Netherlands), and in those which view proliferation as a clear and present danger (such as Italy or Turkey).[22] In 1992, then German Defence Minister Volker Rühe stated publicly that NATO's nuclear weapons 'insure us politically against risks that we cannot calculate, risks which might arise from the proliferation of weapons of mass destruction'.[23] German experts such as Alfred Dregger, Karl-Heinz Kamp and Uwe Nerlich have also written favourably on this subject.[24]

Nevertheless, the use of nuclear weapons to deter WMD is either an unknown concept or associated with extremist theses of nuclear war-fighting. Public consensus will thus not easily be gained. The Gulf War of 1990–91 is the only regional conflict in which the use of nuclear weapons has been discussed; it was ruled out by France and, in a less clear-cut way, by the UK. Precedents matter in managing international crises. There is a danger that, if a regional NBC threat emerged unexpectedly and European governments hinted at the possibility that nuclear weapons could play a part in deterring it, public opposition may ensue, resulting in 'self-deterrence'.

The No-First-Use Question

The no-first-use debate is one of the oldest in the long history of transatlantic nuclear discussion. It was particularly salient in the early 1980s, when four prominent US figures, McGeorge Bundy, George Kennan, Robert McNamara and Gerald Smith, strongly criticised the first-use option in the Spring 1982 issue of *Foreign Affairs*. According to the four, first-use was not credible because US nuclear superiority had disappeared, and because it was based on bluff given the high risk of escalation. It was also dangerous since it encouraged a weak conventional defence and greater reliance on nuclear use, thus increasing the risks of pre-emption. By contrast, adopting a no-first-use pledge would rebuild a nuclear consensus in NATO and help to end the arms race.[25] The Soviet Union exploited the article to remind the world that it had assumed an 'obligation' not to be the first to use nuclear weapons, although it fell short of embracing a true no-first-use doctrine; rather, Moscow would 'naturally take into account how the other nuclear powers act'. In the subsequent issue of *Foreign Affairs*, four German experts rebutted the no-first-use proposal, arguing that such a pledge would allow the Soviets to calculate the risk of aggression against the Alliance, making conflict more likely.[26]

Since the end of the Cold War, an increasing number of Europeans have campaigned in favour of no-first-use. European members of the Canberra Commission strongly supported it. According to Robert O'Neill, conventional aggression by Russia could be deterred by NATO's conventional forces.[27] André Dumoulin predicts that nuclear weapons will increasingly be useful only to deter nuclear use.[28] Roberto Zadra asserts that a no-first-use posture would have important political advantages.[29] The British Labour Party openly favours no-first-use, as does the 'Group of Eight' non-nuclear states, three of which are in Europe.

A major transatlantic debate on the subject has begun. The 1998 SPD–Green 'government contract' mentioned that Germany would campaign for the renunciation of first-use policies. While little attention was paid to this statement, Foreign Minister Joschka Fischer's subsequent declarations to the magazine *Der Spiegel* and other media, indicating his readiness to press the matter, elicited a vigorous and negative reaction from the US administration. The British and French governments also made it publicly known that no-first-use was incompatible with their doctrines.[30] The German Defence Ministry, a traditional guardian of nuclear orthodoxy, sought to downplay the importance of Fischer's statements and reassure the country's Allies.[31] It did not, however, succeed in closing the issue.

The terms of this new debate are different from those of the Cold War. Proponents of no-first-use now argue that using nuclear weapons in response to conventional or WMD aggression would be unnecessary given the significantly superior conventional forces of Alliance countries. In particular, a conventional response to a limited biological or chemical strike would be far more 'proportionate'. Harald Müller, an expert close to German government circles, asserts that European nuclear weapons should now be a 'mere counter-weight to the arsenal remaining in Russia'.[32] No-first-use advocates also point out that the policy would be a stabilising measure since it would make nuclear deterrence more credible, thereby 're-legit-

imising' it. Most importantly, as Fischer noted, no-first-use w<
an important non-proliferation move.

Opponents challenge all of these arguments. While
would agree that there is no massive conventional threat that v
warrant a nuclear response, and that limited biological or chemical
aggression would not necessarily elicit a nuclear strike, they also
question the value of 'conventional deterrence'. A no-first-use
pledge would 'encourage an aggressor to believe he could pursue
conventional aggression to achieve political and territorial gains
without risk of crossing the nuclear threshold'.[33] Conventional
deterrence as a strategic policy has failed countless times in the past,
and costly arms races could result from exclusive reliance on
classical weapons to deter major threats.

Moreover, no-first-use would actually encourage proliferation
because it would signal that a biological or chemical strike would
under no circumstances prompt a nuclear response. Regional
aggressors could then be 'encouraged to believe that the use of
chemical or biological weapons would be a "no-added-cost"
option'.[34] Nuclear weapons have a unique deterrent value rooted in
the fear that they inspire. It is therefore not so much the respective
technical capabilities of conventional and nuclear weapons which
should be taken into account when weighing the merits of each type
of deterrence, but the difference in nature between the two. The fact
that Iraqi President Saddam Hussein did not use biological or
chemical weapons during the Gulf War is seen to support this view.

Opponents of no-first-use also point out that, even if declared,
it would be reversible, and is thus barely credible. As Sir Michael
Quinlan put it in 1997, 'the idea that a nuclear power would let itself
be overwhelmed simply because of a no-first-use promise is plainly
absurd'.[35] Finally, opponents argue that a no-first-use pledge would
undermine the fundamental notion that nuclear weapons are
maintained to deter major aggression in general, whatever its nature,
not just specific threats. No-first-use would take the Allies 'out of the
realm of war prevention and into the realm of war limitation'.[36]

Most European NATO governments remain opposed to no-
first-use.[37] Opposition is particularly strong in France and the UK.
Both countries are keen to emphasise that their nuclear deterrents
cover all threats against their vital interests, whatever the means
employed. Nonetheless, the debate over the issue is only beginning.

NATO doctrine was discussed during an informal ministerial lunch in December 1998, where it was apparently agreed that some debate on Alliance nuclear strategy would take place after the Washington Summit.[38] In the meantime, the Allies would emphasise that the circumstances warranting nuclear use would be 'extremely' rare.

A less controversial option could be the more subtle 'no-first-use of WMD' strategy proposed in 1995 by three RAND analysts, David Gompert, Kenneth Watman and Dean Wilkening.[39] Under this proposal, nuclear weapons would be maintained to deter regional WMD threats, but their first use would be renounced against conventional ones. An option such as this will attract increasing interest in European policy circles. Many German defence experts differentiate between using nuclear weapons against a conventional threat, and using them against a biological or chemical one. Those who oppose no-first-use do so largely on the grounds that it would undermine the capacity to deter a WMD strike on NATO forces or territories.[40] Even those close to government circles seem to take a favourable view of a 'soft' version of no-first-use which would not foreclose using nuclear weapons against WMD. This form of compromise could be a basis on which to update Alliance strategies and reforge a European consensus.

the virtues of pledging no-first-use of WMD

There are also more elaborate options. Current policy could be reaffirmed, but with an addendum making clear that, in present conditions, there is no credible conventional threat warranting a nuclear response. No-first-use against a conventional threat would thus be applicable with a *rebus sic stantibus* clause (that is, it would be valid only as long as conditions did not substantially change). A bolder option would be to embrace a fully fledged no-first-use policy, but with a caveat in case of 'the most extreme circumstances', such as a massive biological attack.

The Future of the NATO Deterrent in Europe

Several issues concerning the future of the NATO deterrent in Europe could prompt contention. The first is the adaptation of NATO nuclear structures and procedures to allow systems and weapons, if necessary, to be moved to an area of crisis, thereby demonstrating Alliance resolve and solidarity. Some European members, for political or financial reasons, may oppose these changes because of the training, basing, infrastructure and computer-software upgrade costs, among others, that they involve. Some states already seem to find it difficult to meet their training and host-nation commitments, and have requested US financial support to help them to discharge their NATO nuclear obligations.[41] According to a 1993 US General Accounting Office (GAO) report, 'the United States spends millions of dollars to provide facilities, equipment, and other support that host nations promised to provide'.[42] In the longer term, further reductions in the permanent presence of US conventional forces could call into question the allocation of a large number of personnel and a significant proportion of defence budgets for nuclear weapons: the Cold War's 'no nukes, no troops' dictum could become 'no troops, no nukes'.

Weapons procurement could also be a source of disagreement. The US nuclear weapon reportedly deployed in Europe – the B-61 – is a multipurpose device with variable yield; several versions, including the B-61-10, date from the 1980s. In contrast with the Cold War, there is today no debate on weapons modernisation. NATO has cited no need to deploy new weapon systems, such as air-launched missiles, and the B-61s, reportedly one of the most reliable weapons in the US arsenal, will not become obsolete for several decades. However, nuclear weapons are kept under constant review as they age. Were a major safety problem to be detected in the B-61s and it became necessary to withdraw them, NATO would be left without nuclear weapons in Europe.[43] Moreover, if the WMD threat became more salient, the 'modernisation' debate might resurface, prompted by the existence of a new version of the B-61 (the B-61-11), which includes an underground penetration capability. This weapon stirred controversy in 1995–96, as some US officials cumbersomely (and wrongly) publicised it as the perfect 'bunker-buster' for counter-proliferation missions. If Alliance officials considered basing this weapon in Europe for deterrence purposes, a careful examination of the political costs and benefits of such a decision would be needed before it was taken.

The presence of the B-61s in Europe is likely to be discussed in the future for a variety of political, budgetary and strategic reasons, including the fact that the US is now the only country to deploy nuclear weapons outside its own territory. Some make the case that the permanent presence of these bombs now serves no purpose, and that there is no clear military need for them. No conventional threat exists in Europe warranting the permanent forward-basing of US nuclear forces; weapons could be relocated to Italy or Turkey if a regional WMD threat emerged, or could even be 'replaced' by extending the sub-strategic *Trident* concept to part of the US submarine-launched capability.[44]

It has been suggested that old arguments, such as 'no nukes, no troops' or that over 'visibility', are no longer relevant to the new strategic environment. For decades, the visibility argument spoke in favour of ground- and air-launched weapons, as opposed to sea-launched ones. It was prominent, for instance, in the thinking of German experts and politicians during the Euromissile crisis in the late 1970s and 1980s, when the option of deploying sea-launched cruise missiles to compensate for Soviet deployments was discussed. But the B-61s are now invisible. Apart from occasional anti-nuclear demonstrations at alleged nuclear sites, they seem to cause little concern and, conversely, provide little reassurance. For the German public, the risk of nuclear war on their soil has dissipated. There is almost no discussion of the B-61s' role, and no one appears to care whether their reported withdrawal from some countries is true or false. The current political value of these weapons for Europeans is therefore in doubt. German experts such as Karl Kaiser judge it more appropriate today to rely on the so-called 'reconstitution' approach – removing peacetime US nuclear deployments, but leaving the option open to deploy weapons in times of crisis.[45] This would also avoid presenting symbolic targets to a future adversary armed with precise ballistic or cruise missiles.

the limited utility of US nuclear weapons in Europe

It is also argued that the political utility of the permanent presence of US weapons is at best limited. Many believe that transatlantic links now lie more in combined operations, such as the Stabilisation Force in the former Yugoslavia. US nuclear weapons in Europe add little to Washington's political influence on the continent. If their primary purpose is to be a vehicle for influence within NATO, some believe that it would be better for the US to prepare for their withdrawal now, rather than be forced to do so later under European pressure. The contribution of these weapons to non-proliferation in Europe might also be marginal. American influence on the continent and non-proliferation depend more on other economic, political, cultural and military factors. It is doubtful that the B-61s are 'the key for diluting both security and non-security motivations for Germany to become a nuclear power', as US Air Force (USAF) Major Mark Gose has claimed, or that the issue is really 'whether there will be US nuclear weapons in Europe – or German ones' as Walter Slocombe argued before joining the Department of Defense.[46]

But this may not be an 'either–or' issue. It may be going too far to suggest that Germany's perceptions of its place in the world would alone dictate whether the country takes the improbable decision to acquire nuclear weapons irrespective of the US nuclear guarantee.[47] However, a more convincing case can be made that 'if 10 or 15 years hence [Germany] is confronted with some new enemy, and if European [integration] has not advanced much and NATO has long since evolved into a hollow shell, German leaders might look at a nuclear arsenal whether or not US nuclear weapons remain on the continent'.[48] But if the B-61s were removed, it seems more likely that Germany would simply 'go further in its habit of redefining extended deterrence by stating that the US nuclear umbrella might be reliable even without American forces deployed on European territory'.[49] South Korea has continued to benefit from the same level of US protection after nuclear weapons were removed from the country in 1992. In Europe, a form of burden-sharing would still be present in the collective decision-making process.[50]

Withdrawing US nuclear weapons would undoubtedly have advantages. It would reflect well on the West's record in Article VI of the NPT – calling for nuclear disarmament – particularly given the increased commitments undertaken at the 1995 NPT Review and Extension Conference. It would foster *détente* with Russia, and would help to delegitimise Moscow's tactical/theatre nuclear weapons.[51] It would also mitigate the risk of creating unwanted political or security threats should a major conflict break out in the southern Balkans, since both Greece and Turkey are believed to host US bombs, and would also erase any perceived differences in status in the Alliance. A final, albeit more debatable, advantage could be to 'bring about an end to the illusion of an automatic enlarged American sanctuary'. It might be salutary for the Alliance as a whole to recognise that the US 'umbrella' now only opens manually, not automatically.[52]

Despite these potential advantages, most European political leaders do not question the US nuclear presence on the continent. Many, particularly in Germany, Italy and Turkey, still see these weapons as tangible evidence of US protection, while even French experts generally approve of their presence as contributing to stability. US nuclear weapons in Europe are sometimes seen as a key to the gradual 'Europeanisation' of NATO doctrine during the Cold War.[53] Moreover, since the US presence ensures physical European participation in nuclear planning and missions, it could be argued that it is a necessary element in the nuclear culture needed to develop a future European deterrent.

It is far from obvious that removing US nuclear weapons would result in a net security gain. Withdrawing them might be perceived as a qualitative jump backwards for the US interest in European security; 'neither the substance nor the symbolism of this new reality would be lost … on potential global adversaries'.[54] Would it be prudent and credible for the Alliance to rely solely on *Trident* for threatening a limited strike, given that it has no visibility, cannot be recalled and is barely available, other than as a complement, for a sub-strategic strike against a major power such as Russia, which would have post-launch detection capabilities allowing it to neutralise the submarine and its remaining SLBM capacity? As for reconstitution, 'having removed nuclear weapons from bases in allied countries, the US might not be able to revive a deterrent role without aggravating the crisis that has occasioned the reappraisal'.[55] The presence of US bombs also contributes to maintaining highly trained air forces in small NATO Europe host countries: 'more than one [dual-capable aircraft]-deploying nation can be expected to do everything possible to retain this mission … since it justifies force structure which otherwise would be cut from active inventories'.[56] Withdrawal might place France in a politically difficult situation since it would become the only Western European country deploying nuclear forces on land. Finally, some US experts warn against the risk of opening the Pandora's box of Alliance strategy, arguing that '[the US] Congress is not ready for a change in nuclear policy in Europe'.[57]

Nuclear Weapons and Alliance Enlargement

Arguments related to nuclear issues and extended deterrence have been used to oppose NATO enlargement. Since the territory of several new or prospective members borders Russia, nuclear escalation in any conflict would immediately and automatically take place on Russian territory (a situation which the US was always reluctant to consider during Cold War debates). This will, supposedly, lessen the credibility of extended deterrence. Second, enlargement will have unwanted effects. It will bolster Russian arguments for greater reliance on nuclear weapons, and also give the Duma a good reason to slow down the arms-control process.[58] Third, the Allies may need to rely more on nuclear weapons in the future as their conventional resources shrink and their commitments grow. This point has been raised by both Russian and Western experts and policy-makers, in particular in rejecting the option of Baltic membership of the Alliance on the grounds that 'NATO could only defend the Baltics by one means, nuclear attacks'.[59] While Russians, who know a weak point in NATO policy when they see one, have sought to manipulate the nuclear question in dealing with enlargement, Moscow's unease on this issue is genuine.[60] The possibility that NATO could base nuclear weapons next to its borders is a long-standing Russian fear, as the controversy in the early 1960s over the presence of *Jupiter* IRBMs in Turkey attests. Finally, extending the nuclear guarantee to new members could also complicate the future admission of neutral or non-aligned countries with well-known nuclear allergies, such as Austria or Sweden.

These arguments suggest that it might be tempting to downgrade the nuclear dimension of Article 5 of the Washington Treaty further if enlargement is to remain a priority. However, nuclear issues have, so far, been smoothly managed, starting with the *Study on NATO Enlargement* issued in September 1995. The study noted that while there was no '*a priori* requirement for the stationing of nuclear weapons on the territory of new members', they 'will be expected to support the concept of deterrence', and 'should be eligible to join the Nuclear Planning Group and its subordinate bodies and to participate in nuclear consultation during exercises and crises'.[61] In the NATO–Russia Founding Act, the Alliance reiterated that it had 'no intention, no plan and no reason to deploy

nuclear weapons on the territory of new members' – the so-called
'Three Nos' – and affirmed that this would also apply to nuclear-
weapon storage sites.[62] Since only a small number of Allies host US
nuclear weapons, stationing weapons on the territory of new
members can hardly be considered a prerequisite if these countries
are to benefit from NATO's collective-security guarantee. This has
allowed Hungary, for instance, to point out that 'there is, and will
continue to be, a single class in NATO, irrespective of the deployment of nuclear weapons'.[63] No new or prospective member is on
record as demanding that nuclear weapons should be stationed on
its territory. Official statements have hinted that doing so could have
political value. On several occasions, Polish leaders have stated that
there was 'no security requirement' for deployment, which could be
interpreted as meaning that nuclear weapons could be welcome as a
political assurance.[64] Havel and Czech Prime Minister Vaclav Klaus
also vaguely raised the possibility of NATO nuclear deployments in
1995–96. But all retreated quickly from their positions, especially
given the lack of public support for them.[65] Most East European
leaders realised early in the enlargement debate that raising this
issue would only complicate their admission.

Since the mid-1990s, an increasing number of experts and
organisations in favour of rapid disarmament, as well as official
proposals from Belarus and Ukraine, with Russian support, have
suggested foreclosing the deployment option by, for example,
establishing a nuclear-weapon-free zone.[66] The Alliance has so far
refused to turn what is today a *de facto* nuclear-weapon-free zone
into a *de jure* one, although some NATO countries view the idea
favourably in principle.[67] NATO members do not foresee any need to
change their policy in the future, but Secretary of Defense William
Cohen made clear to the US Congress in April 1997 that 'implicit in
that statement [the 'Three Nos'] is the fact that the Alliance reserves
the right to reassess this policy if presented with a different security
environment'.[68] A key argument against a nuclear-weapon-free zone
is that it would create differences in status *vis-à-vis* international law
– as opposed to differences in political positions – regarding the
stationing of nuclear weapons. Although some claim that the Two
Plus Four Treaty established a precedent by forbidding the deployment of nuclear weapons in the new German *Länder*, it included a
loophole by leaving the term 'deployment' undefined and subject to

interpretation, perhaps allowing for temporary deployments in a crisis.[69] East Europeans do not seem to welcome being included in a nuclear-weapon-free zone, which they interpret as a sign that they would become 'second-class' members. They also see it as a reminder of the Soviet-inspired Rapacki Plan and other denuclearisation initiatives of the 1950s and 1960s which sought, in essence, to ban US nuclear weapons from Germany. New members have thus taken a careful position. While welcoming the 'Three-Nos' policy, then Polish Foreign Minister Dariusz Rosati remarked in 1997 that: 'This does not mean that if the situation changes, it won't be possible to deploy these weapons. Let's recall, the Alliance has not undertaken any formal obligation'.[70]

Any future commitment never to deploy nuclear weapons east of the Oder–Neiße, whatever form it took, could not be called off at short notice. To deploy nuclear weapons, even on a temporary basis without storage, would probably require important command, control and communications work on East European air bases to enable them to host US nuclear weapons with NATO standards. This work would not perhaps go unnoticed. Even though such developments would not be formally precluded by the NATO–Russia Founding Act, Russia need not fear an abrupt reversal of NATO policy in this area.

Arms Control: What Role for France and the UK?

France and the UK were at the forefront of the 1995 NPT talks and subsequent CTBT negotiations, and have strongly pressed for the early establishment of a fissile-material cut-off regime. Both have greatly reduced their nuclear forces since the end of the Cold War, and have announced detargeting. London and Paris provide Russia with technical assistance in dismantling its weapons. France has engaged in a cooperative programme ('AIDA-MOX') to reprocess used Russian fuels; the UK has taken important measures in the field of fissile-material transparency.

Despite these activities, there is no realistic prospect that either France or the UK will give up their nuclear deterrent in the near future. In a 1998 speech, Jospin stated that 'for France, as for European security, and as long as general and complete disarmament will not be achieved, nuclear weapons will remain necessary'.[71] Neither London nor Paris is likely to join the US–Russian arms-reduction process in the near future. It could be argued that there is no legitimate rationale for this continued abstention now that the 'superpowers' have dramatically reduced their own arsenals – a precondition traditionally put forward by Paris and London. From the British or French point of view, however, this fails to take into account several key elements. First, both countries have unilaterally reduced their own arsenals to a point, in relative terms, equivalent to the cuts made by the US and Russia.

no prospect of France or the UK giving up nuclear weapons

Second, US and Russian arsenals are still significantly larger than those of the UK and France, especially considering the actual total of nuclear weapons currently in their inventories, as opposed to START-accountable warhead targets. Thus, the UK SDR stated that 'considerable further reductions [in US and Russian arsenals] would be needed before further British reductions could become feasible'.[72] Third, both countries consider their own deterrents as 'sufficient' or 'minimum', not determined by the size of other nuclear powers' arsenals. According to French Defence Minister Alain Richard, US and Russian force sizes are still 'configured according to a logic of mutual neutralisation'.[73] Finally, both France and the UK have seen additional reasons for caution since the end of the Cold War in the uncertainty surrounding the future of the non-proliferation regime and, most importantly, the Anti-Ballistic Missile (ABM) Treaty, which is viewed as a guarantee of strategic stability. A US decision to deploy an NMD system would not improve the chances of British and French participation in multilateral arms reductions, since both London and Paris fear that such a system would in the long term indirectly affect their own penetration capabilities against other countries.

For France and the UK to participate in the arms-reduction process, a number of conditions would need to be met. These include further verified nuclear reductions by Russia and the US; maintaining the NPT and ABM regimes; and Chinese participation simultaneous with theirs. Even so, critical questions would emerge. How would the smaller, 'non-official' arsenals of other countries be taken into account? What would be the goal sought by 'P-5' negotiations between the Security Council Permanent Members? Proportionate reductions for all would assume that the value of one nuclear weapon is constant whatever the size of the arsenal, a notion that China, France and the UK would certainly challenge. But an identical fixed target or ceiling for each of the five (100–200 warheads, for example) would imply that the US and Russia would bear the brunt of reductions, and might not be compatible with the continued existence of the US extended deterrent.

In the meantime, there are prospects for serious cooperation among the P-5 states, notably in the NPT Enhanced Review Process. This could lead to further arms-control measures, such as a formal detargeting regime. The multilateralisation of existing agreements such as the INF or ABM treaties might also be considered. Further unilateral steps in the field of transparency or alert levels are not precluded either. However, extreme 'de-alerting' measures, such as 'de-mating' warheads and missiles, are likely to be opposed by France and the UK, which consider them to be irrelevant to, or incompatible with, their deterrence postures.

There are risks of significant disagreements between allies over the adaptation of nuclear strategies. The consensus on maintaining deterrence against a residual or emerging nuclear threat, and the preservation of some sharing of risks and responsibilities within NATO to sustain this deterrent, is probably not in danger. But key issues must now be re-examined in light of the emergence of more limited threats: the exact scope of nuclear deterrence; the details of Alliance strategy; and the balance between deterrence, defences and arms control. This may result in increasing tensions between NATO allies, among European countries, or between Europe and the US.

chapter 4

Developing a European Nuclear Identity

The political role of US nuclear weapons in Europe is long-standing, supposedly fostering Alliance cohesion and coupling the US to Europe. But a second, emerging political role concerns only British and French nuclear weapons. For some, these arms could be instruments of European political autonomy, including in relation to the US, and could promote a general European defence identity. The challenge for Alliance countries, in particular the three nuclear powers, will be to maintain the transatlantic link while developing some form of European 'nuclear identity', resulting in a net political and security gain.

European Integration and the Nuclear Issue

On several occasions since the mid-1980s, Europeans have engaged in dialogue on nuclear issues. The Hague Platform, adopted in 1987 by the WEU Council of Ministers in the midst of the Euromissile crisis and following the US–Soviet Reykjavik Summit, was a milestone in this area. While the allies deviated little from NATO-validated concepts – reaffirming the importance of nuclear deterrence, the role of US nuclear forces in Europe and the contribution of British and French nuclear forces – the Platform was remarkable in that it was a strictly European forum, held at a time when the Reagan administration was expressing doubts about its attachment to nuclear deterrence.[1] Discussion has also taken place on nuclear non-proliferation issues in the WEU. The WEU Council of Ministers meetings in Noordwijk in the Netherlands in November 1994 and in Madrid in November 1995 adopted seminal texts on European security interests, including their nuclear dimension. The NPT Review and Extension Conference in 1995 – the occasion of an EU 'joint action' – was also important in developing common nuclear policies within the Union. EU members have also worked closely together to reinforce the International Atomic Energy Agency (IAEA), and the Union has set up a permanent civilian working group on nuclear issues linked to the European Atomic Energy Community (Euratom).[2] With the exception of Austria, Ireland and Sweden, all EU members generally vote together on nuclear issues in the UN General Assembly. In addition, since the early 1990s the European Parliament has tackled nuclear-weapon issues, and has organised seminars and hearings on the subject.

France has taken the lead in promoting further European cooperation on nuclear issues. On 10 January 1992, Mitterrand unexpectedly raised the issue of a common European nuclear doctrine, stating that it would 'quickly become one of the major questions in the construction of a common European defence'.[3] There is general consensus in this area in France. Although the term *dissuasion concertée* was coined by a Socialist, then Junior Defence Minister Jacques Mellick, in 1992, Gaullists have strongly promoted the idea.[4] In September 1995, Juppé stated that 'we should learn to make the collective dimension an integral part of our doctrine'.[5] The 1997–2002 Six-Year Defence Plan reinforced the message by stating that 'with the other European countries, the implementation, in the long run, of a common defence as planned by the Treaty on the European Union calls for a *concertation* [on deterrence]'.[6] Although Socialist experts have been more cautious on this issue than their centre-right counterparts, they do not question the belief that nuclear issues will increasingly have a European dimension. Before becoming Foreign Minister, Védrine was keen to emphasise, as Mitterrand had done, that there would be no European deterrent without common vital interests, and that it should come only as a final step in European construction – but he did not challenge the utility of *concertation*.[7] Other Socialists have criticised the timing of the initiative, but not its principles.[8] Jospin confirmed in September 1997 that France wants to

thinking seriously about
dissuasion concertée

'deepen the dialogue with its main partners on the whole range of questions pertaining to deterrence'.[9]

France does not intend to replace the NATO deterrent, but would like it to have a specifically European dimension. The idea is to draw the logical conclusion from the growing solidarity between European countries. Economic and political integration and the free flow of people, goods, information and capital are making the existence, security and well-being of European nations ever more dependent upon each other. European vital interests are increasingly intertwined, and the old French idea that 'the nuclear risk cannot be shared' is increasingly judged to be obsolete.[10] Nuclear weapons are viewed as a key to Europe's strategic autonomy, without which European integration will be incomplete. Furthermore, lessening the differences in nuclear status in Europe could be valuable by preventing them from becoming potential obstacles to integration; nuclear 'have-not' states could become 'have-a-little' ones within a future single political entity. This is a pragmatic approach, gradually promoting increased nuclear solidarity among interested EU countries in a way more akin to a process than a blueprint.[11] According to Chirac:

> *This is not about unilaterally extending our deterrence or imposing a new contract on our partners. This is about drawing all the consequences from a community of destiny, of a growing and intertwining of our vital interests. Taking into account the difference in sensitivity that exists in Europe about nuclear weapons, we do not propose a ready-made concept, but a gradual process, open to those partners who wish to join.[12]*

This implies that France increasingly takes the rest of the EU into account in nuclear-policy decisions that could affect its partners. Indications of this new French policy include the Anglo-French declaration on shared vital interests in November 1995, the expressed readiness to discuss nuclear issues in the North Atlantic Council (NAC) in December 1995, the declared intent to terminate the *Hadès* SRBM in consultation with Germany in February 1996, and the agreement on opening dialogue with Germany on nuclear deterrence in December 1996.

French ideas have been met with scepticism elsewhere in Europe. Some viewed them as a means to sweeten the bitter pill of nuclear testing. However, Juppé had first mentioned the *dissuasion concertée* idea in a major policy speech in January 1995, before it had been decided that testing should be resumed: 'After the elaboration of a doctrine common to France and Great Britain, must our generation shy away from contemplating, not a shared deterrent, but at the minimum a *dissuasion concertée* with our main partners?'.[13] Chirac had emphasised the European dimension of nuclear deterrence on several occasions before becoming president in 1995.[14] Others have criticised the timing of French ideas given the current state of European integration. When chairing the European Council of Ministers in 1996, Javier Solana argued that 'dealing with nuclear issues from the outset is like starting to build a house from the roof down'.[15] It also appears that the echoes of the European nuclear debates of the 1970s and 1980s still reverberate. In Germany, Italy and Spain, many in the political classes were relieved that nuclear issues had disappeared, and were not interested in reopening the debate unless compelled to do so. Probably a stronger argument against the French initiatives is that most countries have declared themselves satisfied with current NATO arrangements, and do not see the immediate need for a *concertation* on nuclear deterrence.

This is the case in the UK, where the view is widespread that what France is suggesting already exists within NATO. But British officials and experts, who are keen to recall that UK forces already protect Europe through the NATO collective deterrent, are nevertheless generally open to discussing the principle of a European *concertation* on nuclear issues. Although more reluctant than France to pursue deeper European integration in general, London has been much more at ease than Paris in recognising common vital interests in Europe. It took three years – and a change in leadership – for France publicly to agree, through the November 1995 declaration, that there were such shared interests, a view suggested by the British government as early as 1992. In general, the British position on *dissuasion concertée* is that it is 'welcomed' as long as it has a double dimension, European and Atlantic.[16]

Germany has also been cautious. Several CDU figures – Alfred Dregger, Karl Lamers, Friedbert Pflüger and Wolfgang Schaüble, for example – have stated that they would support the idea of a European dialogue on nuclear matters, and would welcome a European contribution as a 'complement' or 'reinforcement' of the US commitment, or as a 'support' to the European pillar of NATO in the conventional field.[17] Karl-Heinz Kamp has argued that 'a European Union capable of forging a common currency can hardly exclude its national nuclear posture from common considerations'.[18] Others have welcomed the idea of a nuclear discussion as a catalyst for a broader domestic debate on security needs, and on Germany's attitudes towards nuclear weapons.[19] However, some wish to avoid tackling such divisive issues, believing that doing so could be counterproductive for the European political debate, or the national defence debate.[20] Others reject the French initiatives as being rooted in national self-interest.[21] Some have even insisted that European nuclear discussions 'could only mean that the countries of Europe jointly organize the abandonment of nuclear weapons'.[22] (Volker Rühe himself wanted to see British and French systems included in discussions of START III.)[23] The SPD–Green government has not refused to tackle the European nuclear issue, but would prefer the debate to be deferred to a later stage of European integration.[24]

There is also concern in German policy circles that growing European cooperation on nuclear deterrence could prompt an unwanted downgrading of the US nuclear guarantee, or lead to a questioning of the US nuclear presence in the country. In 1995, Rühe stressed that 'nothing can replace NATO's nuclear umbrella'.[25] As defence analysts Holger Mey and Andrew Denison put it, 'cooperation with France must not be allowed to jeopardize the nuclear protection offered by the United States'.[26] There is also concern that Germany's increased European nuclear cooperation could, outside the country, be taken to indicate a willingness to move its hand closer to Europe's two nuclear buttons. At the same time, the question of the country's international status is no longer taboo. Germany might consider that reducing the difference in status between itself and France and the UK would be an asset in the debate on reforming the UN Security Council.

Southern European countries have shown some interest in French ideas. Italian support for multinational deterrence concepts is long-standing, and several Italian analysts have written in favour of increased European nuclear cooperation.[27] While 'Europeanists' seem to have lost ground in Rome's defence policy-making circles, strong interest in the concept persists among leading analysts such as Carlo Jean and Giuseppe Cucchi.[28] Some Spanish defence analysts close to government circles have written positively on European deterrence.[29] Benelux countries, traditionally pioneers of European integration, are also receptive to the concept, and to the idea that the vital interests of European countries are increasingly intertwined.[30] The French ideas have occasionally met with an interested, and in some cases sympathetic, response in Central and Eastern Europe.[31] However, most countries there either share Germany's cautious approach to any moves that could weaken transatlantic links, or place the French initiative in the broader context of a supposed rivalry between France and the US within NATO.

Northern European countries, where strong anti-nuclear sentiment is combined with reluctance to consider a common European defence policy, have most adamantly opposed cooperation on nuclear issues, while Ireland is also sensitive about it. In 1994, Norway was deeply reluctant about making specific references to nuclear deterrence in WEU texts for fear that doing so would undermine public approval of the country's entry into the EU. Oslo is not ready to open a new nuclear debate. Sweden claims that Europeans should take the lead in disarmament, rather than promote new nuclear concepts, and overtly opposes a dialogue on nuclear deterrence. Denmark and Finland, which frequently vote differently from the other neutral and non-aligned countries on nuclear issues in multinational fora, remain sceptical.

Prospects for European Dialogue and Cooperation

It is clear that French ideas are unlikely to be developed quickly or fully, especially since French leaders themselves want to move cautiously. It could be argued that, far from being, as Solana put it, the 'roof' of a European common defence policy, the nuclear dimension could be its 'foundation': that agreement on security's last resort would assist cooperation on other defence issues. However, in current political and strategic conditions there is no need to move speedily on this issue.

The Franco-German Strategic Concept adopted by Chirac and Kohl in December 1996 highlighted how sensitive nuclear issues remain in Europe.[32] The Concept included two short and seemingly innocuous sentences on nuclear deterrence in the midst of a 20-page document devoted essentially to political–military issues and bilateral conventional cooperation. However, because the text, which was supposed to be kept secret until both parliaments had read and discussed it, was leaked to the French newspaper *Le Monde*, the 'nuclear paragraph' became the focus of intense interest. In the US and other Allied countries, officials and experts speculated over what the French and Germans intended in announcing that 'our countries are ready to engage in a dialogue concerning the role of nuclear deterrence, in the context of European defence policy'.[33] In the French parliament, many members declared that they were shocked by the language used, according to which 'the supreme guarantee of the security of the Allies is assured by the strategic forces of the Alliance, in particular those of the United States', before mentioning the specific role of British and French nuclear weapons.[34]

In Germany, Rühe claimed that 'for the first time, France signed a document in which NATO nuclear defence holds the decisive place'. In fact, this wording was simply taken from the 1974 Ottawa Alliance Summit Declaration.[35] But in the eyes of some French experts, such as Socialist Party defence spokesman Paul Quilès, it was 'unacceptable in a European text'.[36] It seems that the Concept became the subject of intense discussion because it was rightly seen as inseparable from the debate over France's relationship with the Alliance. Thus, German insistence on placing future bilateral nuclear dialogue in a general Alliance context – which would make it acceptable in Germany – collided with French Socialist and nationalist sensitivities about the country's *rapprochement* with NATO.[37]

This bilateral dialogue will be a slow and sensitive process, and is unlikely to develop quickly into a strong nuclear relationship. But there are grounds for agreement. In July 1997, Quilès and his German counterpart Günter Verheugen issued a joint statement – 'France and Germany: Partners in Europe and for Europe' – which suggested establishing a European nuclear-consultation group, and acknowledged that Germany should not interfere in French national decisions on nuclear disarmament.[38] It seems that, if European nuclear discussions are to be acceptable, they should not be limited to deterrence policy and strategy, but should also include non-proliferation, disarmament and missile defences. An incremental approach would therefore probably be preferable, building on existing discussions on fissile-material trafficking, the control of dual-use technology and WMD proliferation. Discussions of the post-Cold War role of nuclear weapons could then follow. The nuclear element's place in European integration, and the possible European roles of British and French forces, would be tackled only after these issues had been addressed.

Where should European nuclear discussions take place? French expert Frédéric Bozo has suggested merging the Anglo-French and Franco-German dialogues into a trilateral nuclear commission.[39] However, the nature of these discussions is different, and merging them could be misinterpreted by other European nations – Italy for instance – as creating a European nuclear 'directorate'. Nuclear cooperation in Europe could not function as it does within NATO, where one country – the US – is legitimately seen as first among equals. Discussion of nuclear-deterrence issues in a formal EU setting is unlikely, since the Union includes a large number of neutral and non-aligned countries opposed to the idea. EU enlargement will make formal dialogue on these issues even more difficult.[40] A more fruitful approach may be informal discussion with all interested countries in an *ad hoc* institutional framework, possibly under WEU auspices. This option, which could make it easier to involve not only 'core' European countries but also some prospective East European members of the EU, has some political support in parliamentary circles, while the WEU Assembly has adopted a number of recommendations and reports to this effect.[41]

where should European nuclear discussions take place?

A key step would be to develop a European nuclear doctrine – a detailed text, along the lines of NATO guidelines, drafted by Europeans themselves. The convergence of French and British doctrines makes this possible, since both agree on fundamental principles, such as protecting 'vital interests' and being able to inflict 'unacceptable damage' to deter an adversary. A common European text on nuclear doctrine could have not only political value, but also important practical consequences if it included provisions for European-only nuclear planning and consultation during a crisis. However, Europeans would find it difficult to agree on principles that differed substantially from those underpinning the Alliance deterrent as a whole. It is hard, for instance, to imagine Europeans agreeing to a no-first-use doctrine in the face of US opposition. On the other hand, Europeans might be keen to emphasise the need for strong and swift nuclear retaliation directly against an adversary's territory. This was always a controversial subject in Cold War NATO debates, because the US was more cautious for fear of risking a counter-strike on its own territory.[42]

In one area – follow-on use – any European nuclear doctrine could differ from that of NATO. There has been contention on this issue between France and the UK (and thus between France and NATO). According to British officials, 'there is a follow-on use after substrategic employment of nuclear weapons, while the French do not allow for a follow-on use between substrategic employment, which they intend to be the final warning, and the holocaust'.[43] If this is still the case, a European doctrine would have to choose between French and UK/NATO conceptions. Alternatively, it could leave the option open at this point, or make clear that European countries would intend the first 'sub-strategic' use of nuclear weapons to be the last. While the issue of a European doctrine is thus linked with the broader political issue of the relationship between France and NATO, this point is not as salient as it was in the past. British officials are keen to emphasise the 'clear convergence of thinking' between France and the UK on these concepts.[44] The French have stopped stressing alleged fundamental differences between NATO doctrine and their own.

A European nuclear doctrine taking account of these various European sensibilities could potentially take the following form:

> **1** Nuclear weapons are for deterrence purposes only and can under no circumstances be considered as war-fighting weapons. Only common vital European interests are protected by European nuclear weapons; the independence and integrity of the EU, its territory and population feature prominently among these vital interests.[45]
>
> **2** The role of nuclear weapons is to deter all possible forms of aggression against European vital interests, whatever the means employed. It is not exclusively limited to deterrence against nuclear weapons, although this is an essential function. In the present strategic context, no conventional threat is

perceived that would warrant a nuclear response.

3 Deterrence would be achieved by threatening an adversary with strong and swift nuclear retaliation on its own territory, inflicting unacceptable damage and targeting those assets most highly valued. Nuclear options more limited in scope could be envisaged for situations where an adversary had misjudged European resolve, and to ensure that deterrence would be credible whatever the nature and scope of the threat against European vital interests. The aim of a more limited strike would be to convince the adversary of this resolve, to defend vital interests, to restore deterrence and to cause an adversary to stop its aggression.

4 The fundamental principles of international law, including self-defence, would be applicable to any use of nuclear weapons.

5 While the authority to use nuclear weapons ultimately remains in the hands of nuclear powers, the use of these weapons to defend common interests would require prior consultation between all countries concerned.

A 'European Deterrent'?

A common doctrine would give credence to the idea of Europeans exercising by themselves some form of deterrence in common, as an addition or a complement to the US/NATO one. Building a true European deterrent would mean some type of nuclear operational cooperation among states, and would represent a much more important step forward.

Several arguments have been given in support of building a European deterrent:

- that it would be the ultimate step in European defence integration;
- that, in the long term, only a common European deterrent could ensure that no non-nuclear European country would be tempted to acquire nuclear weapons; and
- that it would make credible the 'supplementary' nature of European nuclear protection by creating a 'second centre of decision', thus transposing this British concept into a European framework.

This last argument is probably the most persuasive. In the eyes of an adversary, there could be situations in which the US nuclear guarantee would not apply. European 'supplementary' protection would, however, persuade an adversary that, even if the US hesitated, Europe would not do so if its vital interests were at stake.[46] With the end of the Cold War, threats against Europe will be more limited in character and scope than in the past; for those who doubt whether US protection can be taken for granted in all circumstances, there is a strong incentive to consider acquiring an additional insurance policy. More broadly, the possession of a nuclear arsenal by Europe as a whole would also guarantee greater freedom of action in international affairs. France and the UK found this reasoning persuasive in deciding to build national deterrent forces in the aftermath of the 1956 Suez *débâcle*, when both countries faced pressure from the US and the Soviet Union to withdraw from Egypt.

The idea of a European deterrent has a long history. It was promoted in particular in the 1950s and 1960s, until truly collective nuclear structures and procedures in NATO were set up under the Kennedy administration.[47] Trilateral operational cooperation between France, Germany and Italy began in the 1950s, but was halted when Charles de Gaulle took power in 1958. The debates over a NATO Multilateral Force and over the NPT in the early 1960s prompted some thinking about a future European deterrent. Both Germany and Italy included reservations in their NPT Ratification Acts, some of them aimed at ensuring that the Treaty would not preclude developing a European political and security entity.[48]

France and the UK have long given some thought to a European deterrent. For the British, a wider European role for nuclear forces is not a conceptual problem in itself – as long as it is in an Alliance context – since the UK considers that its vital interests would be threatened to the point of warranting a nuclear response if those of one of its NATO allies were endangered.[49] Thus, the idea of an overt role for British and French forces in protecting Europe tends to be viewed favourably, along with the country's more balanced attitude to its security relations with Europe on the one hand, and the US on the other.[50] For France, the idea of common vital interests is also not that new, despite the country's image of 'splendid isolation' during the Cold War. In 1964, for example, de Gaulle is reported to have instructed his Defence Staff that 'France should feel threatened as soon as the territories of the FRG [West Germany] and Benelux are violated'.[51] Given the country's past policies, it is noteworthy that France has come to admit that there could be a transatlantic dimension to a European deterrent, thus alleviating British concerns. Then Prime Minister Edouard Balladur reported in 1994 that the Anglo-French Joint Commission had established four prerequisites for such a European deterrent: a common concept of deterrence; common vital interests; shared roles and responsibilities; and close cooperation with the US.[52] The 1997–2002 Defence Plan clearly stated that European cooperation on deterrence 'implies also a dialogue with the United States and within the Alliance'.[53]

The combination of a more EU-minded UK and a more NATO-minded France has made possible significant steps such as the 1998 Saint Malo Declaration. The UK's abandonment of its air-launched nuclear capacity could be a further incentive for operational *rapprochement* with France. The gradual development of an Anglo-French European nuclear-deterrent core could ultimately lead to the creation of a single virtual nuclear power, with 'two fingers on the button' in the defence of common interests, in the first or second decade of the twenty-first century. Joint development of next-generation launchers and missiles could be considered although, as far as nuclear technologies are concerned, doing so would require agreement with the US given the depth of UK–US cooperation in this field. Europe would have to choose between what

steps towards a European nuclear force

Sir Michael Quinlan has dubbed Mark I independence (the French model, including procurement independence) and Mark II (the UK model, limited to operational independence).[54] Both political and financial criteria would determine such a choice.

What would a European deterrent look like? Several possible models can be suggested, forming a 'ladder' of possibilities in coming decades. Climbing from one model to another would represent crossing a significant political threshold in each case.

A 'mutualised' deterrent. The first model could be a 'mutualised' deterrent, including: a reaffirmed mutual-defence commitment in an EU context, which would also encompass an explicit nuclear dimension; a formal European 'nuclear-policy

Table 2 *Models for a European Deterrent*

Possible timeframe			
2000–2005	**2005–2010**	**2010–2020**	**Possibly at a later date**
Concept			
Mutualised deterrent	Common deterrent	Joint deterrent	Single deterrent
Multilateral Institutions			
Policy committee	Planning and consultation committee	Multinational command	Single command
Nuclear Forces			
Anglo-French joint targeting options	Anglo-French pooled force, single targeting plan(s)	Next generation of forces developed in common	Single force
Participation of Non-Nuclear Countries			
Policy-making, consultation over use	Risk- and responsibility-sharing (dual-capable aircraft)	Development of missiles, negative veto over use	n.a.
Authority to Use Nuclear Weapons in a European Context			
National	National or joint Anglo-French	Collective (non-nuclear countries have negative veto)	Single federal authority

committee' in the WEU, where non-nuclear nations would participate in policy planning; and stronger Anglo-French operational cooperation and coordination, including joint targeting plans. In the short to medium term, this is not an unrealistic prospect.

A 'common' deterrent. The second model could go beyond the arrangements that currently exist in NATO. A 'common' deterrent would accompany a mutual commitment to common defence, and could include a formal European nuclear-planning and consultation committee and a 'pooling' of French and British forces. In operational terms, these forces would become virtually inseparable (including full coordination of submarine patrols), thereby making joint decisions on nuclear use inevitable, even though each country could retain nominal control over its own portion of the force. All interested members would share costs, risks and responsibilities, including arming some of their aircraft with French Enhanced ASMP missiles, while at the same time retaining the capacity to carry US bombs. Aside from the necessity for two separate security standards and inspections, this dual capacity would not present major technical difficulties. The protection of SSBN patrol zones would be shared.

This model would not necessarily face the same dilemmas as those encountered by NATO in building its own collective deterrent. Instead of being dominated by one major external power, the European deterrent would be built around the forces of two continental medium-sized ones. It would not be formed in reaction to a specific, immediate threat, but to complete a political project. The existence of the EU would more easily foster a shared perception of risks and interests, including by mere proximity. This is a point recognised by British experts such as Beatrice Heuser: 'London and Paris are geographically closer to Berlin and Rome than Washington, and thus more likely to feel implicated by an attack on their neighbours'.[55]

A 'joint' deterrent. The third model, a 'joint' deterrent, would represent a major step forward. It would include joint Anglo-French decision-making on nuclear use, with a negative veto from non-nuclear-weapon states; a 'fused' Anglo-French force with mixed crews on SSBNs; jointly developed missiles; a multinational command; and a single targeting plan. If Europe were to move towards such a model, legal issues would have to be examined. The NPT prohibits the transfer of nuclear weapons to non-nuclear powers; some NGOs have claimed that current NATO procedures allowing for European aircraft to carry US nuclear weapons in times of crisis are contrary to at least the spirit, if not the letter, of the Treaty. Although this analysis is arguable since the release of these weapons would be subject to a formal US presidential decision, any model that went beyond current NATO practice could be obstructed by the NPT. In Germany, the 'Two Plus Four' Treaty could also present difficulties, assuming it was strictly interpreted. However, there are ambiguities. Both Germany and Italy ratified the NPT with the proviso that it would not preclude developing a European union. (The US reportedly assured Germany at the time that a European federal state would not be bound by the NPT.)[56] These legal aspects were examined again in German government circles when the NPT was indefinitely extended in 1995 and, in 1997, Bonn reaffirmed that it did not preclude developing 'a European Union with adequate competences'.[57] Nevertheless, this issue is potentially sensitive. Russia could be concerned that such a form of European deterrent may provide an opportunity for Germany to enter the nuclear club by the back door. These debates were meant to be closed in the late 1960s by the NPT and the simultaneous establishment of truly collective nuclear decision-making in NATO. In light of these political constraints, a collective European deterrent along these lines would be set up only if Europe considered doing so an absolute requirement for its security.

A 'single' deterrent. Under the fourth and final model, a 'single' deterrent, a European federal authority would control an integrated European nuclear force with a single command. European countries could together develop the next generation of submarines, manned by multinational European crews. There is little prospect that this will be implemented in the foreseeable future. Nonetheless, it would be easier to manage than the previous model because only one state, not two, would be involved. Since this would reduce the number of nuclear powers in Europe, the 'NPT obstacle' would be largely irrelevant.

Both political and operational criteria would be involved in judging the credibility of a European deterrent. In relation to Eastern Europe, such a deterrent might be more credible than NATO's since it would be based on more solid geographic, economic and political links, including EU membership. As US expert David Yost put it in 1993, 'with the expansion of East European ties with Western European institutions, it might become clear to Russia that the participating states of Eastern Europe had become a "vital interest" of the [EU] and WEU, and thus the British and French nuclear deterrents might provide them with some protection'.[58] Those Central and Eastern European countries entering the Union will be offered membership of the Brussels Treaty, currently binding on ten NATO-European nations, which includes a mutual-defence agreement with an obligation to resort to military means.

From an operational point of view, according to concepts of minimum deterrence, rather than nuclear 'battle' with multiple strategic exchanges, the combined strength of British and French forces should be considered more than sufficient to deter any major threat. France and the UK already assume that their national deterrents individually have the capacity to inflict unacceptable damage on a major power. The permanent presence at sea of at least two European SSBNs and the deployment of up to six in a crisis, with a total of up to 96 missiles each, would guarantee a much higher degree of survivability than either country could individually enjoy. It would also make it possible to face multiple threats. Even leading US experts have recognised that 'the French and British systems should be sufficient to deter any credible threats from a weakened Russia, or from others'.[59]

However, a credible European deterrent might require the combined fire-power of both countries if it were based on the long-standing notion of 'proportionate' deterrence, that is, where the damage that can be inflicted on an aggressor's territory is equivalent to what is at stake in the conflict – Europe itself. If this deterrent was not based on concepts of proportionality, the combined forces of the UK and France could result in 'surplus' fire-power, and the total number of British and French warheads could be reduced, perhaps by 'cocooning' one SSBN from each country. Creating a European deterrent could thus result in a reduction in European nuclear arsenals.

Another criticism is based on the UK's supposed technological dependence on the US, which would, in turn, mean that a European deterrent would have to rely on external technological inputs, which could theoretically be cut off at any time. But British officials point out that, in the unlikely event that this dependence materialised, 'UK forces would remain operationally viable for a sufficient period to allow alternative arrangements to be put in place'.[60] Should the European nuclear powers need to resume testing, they would depend on the US since the French Pacific test range has been closed; this is, however, unlikely for the foreseeable future.

Other doubts have been raised concerning the ability of European forces to perform limited or selective nuclear strikes.[61] However, as far as the forces themselves are concerned, the UK has publicly declared that its *Trident* system is capable of carrying out sub-strategic strikes, which are by nature selective and limited. France maintains a significant air-based nuclear capacity, including on the *Charles de Gaulle*, which is undoubtedly able to perform limited strikes.

Could Two Multinational Deterrents Coexist?

Assuming that US extended deterrence continues, creating a European nuclear force could give NATO two deterrents, both of which would be approximately the same size in numerical terms. As Europe assumes an increased role in guaranteeing its own security, it would become possible to envisage a new transatlantic arrangement in which the European contribution would be at the fore – a sort of 'Ottawa in reverse', as suggested by one expert, referring to the 1974 declaration recognising the role of the British and French deterrents for Alliance security.[62] However, for operational and technical reasons, such as chains of command and the timing of consultations, it might be difficult for the NATO collective deterrent to coexist with a European one. As Sir Christopher Mallaby, a former British Ambassador to France, suggested in 1996, 'the installation of a double circuit of consultation for the possible opening of nuclear fire for the defence of Europe ... entails potential risks and insta-bilities'.[63] It is not certain that the Western part of the continent is large enough for two collective deterrents. Assuming that the US nuclear presence remains unchanged, a truly European deterrent may be unrealistic. However, this would not be the case if the US were significantly to modify the shape or format of its nuclear commitment to Europe by withdrawing weapons, overtly and publicly downgrading its nuclear guarantee or making a significant doctrinal change such as a no-first-use pledge. Moves such as these would in all likelihood foster a European drive to build a separate deterrent.

The European and NATO dimensions of this 'Eurobomb' problem are thus interdependent since changes on one side could precipitate developments on the other. One view in Europe is that a European deterrent would be necessary only if the US deterrent proved unreliable in the face of emerging new threats. Thus, to a certain extent, developing a European nuclear identity could be facilitated by modifications in the US extended deterrent. On the other hand, maintaining the US nuclear umbrella could also make it easier for Europeans to develop their own nuclear identity, since they would be doing so under continued US protection.

Europeans could think of a European deterrent as a 'precautionary measure' in case the US modified the scope of this protection. As one Italian expert puts it, 'nobody knows how long the US nuclear guarantee will last. The existence of a European nuclear capacity is thus necessary'.[64] However, creating a European nuclear identity could itself encourage American disengagement.

a European deterrent and uncertain US strategy The US Congress, for instance, could argue that the country's nuclear presence and guarantee could be significantly reduced, or even abandoned. For most Europeans today, strategic autonomy is not worth the price of a major transatlantic rift.

It is impossible to separate this issue from the general problem of adapting Alliance structures and procedures. Some modest steps could reflect the emergence of a European nuclear pillar in the Alliance's decision-making system. The HLG and the DPG could be merged into a single group co-chaired by the US and a WEU member-country in rotation. Within NATO's integrated military command structure, the situation might be more complex, but perhaps the Deputy SACEUR, which will represent the European defence and security identity, could have a role in this respect. Also, a European representation at US Strategic Command (STRATCOM) in Nebraska could be envisaged, to optimise coordination and 'deconfliction' in deterrence planning for possible joint action.[65] The question of a European deterrent is also inextricably linked with that of France's relationship with NATO. Since France would be one of the two nuclear powers supporting such a deterrent, and since some form of coordination or information mechanism would have to be set up with the US and NATO, creating a European deterrent would require increased French participation in NATO structures and procedures. If these challenges were met, developing a European deterrent could be a positive step for the Alliance. It could compensate for a perceived or real erosion of the US nuclear guarantee. It would also bolster global deterrence in an enlarged NATO and would bring French assets – the air-launched ASMP missile or carrier-based nuclear capacity which the US gave up in 1994 – into a multinational framework. These could be useful tools in nuclear crisis management. It is even possible that a French nuclear-aircraft presence in NATO could take the place vacated by the British in 1998.

'European deterrence' is a catch-all term, under which different forms and concepts can be developed, from informal political dialogue to strong operational cooperation. European comments and reactions to these issues often confuse very different concepts and possibilities. The idea of a European dimension of deterrence is opposed today by strange bedfellows, 'an unnatural alliance between the atlanticists and the antinuclearists'.[66] However, if it is properly managed and tackled at the appropriate time, 'Euro-peanising' nuclear forces could be a way to maintain the political consensus on nuclear deterrence in Europe, and perhaps lay the foundations for a rebalanced transatlantic partnership.[67]

The end of the Cold War is forcing European governments to review the role of nuclear weapons on the continent. Despite the global reduction of nuclear arsenals, potential new roles – or, rather, new dimensions of old roles – have emerged: to protect former Warsaw Pact nations against Russia; to deter regional WMD aggression; and to help Europe to gain its strategic autonomy. These new roles have supplemented, not replaced, traditional ones, which are still judged valid by European governments: to deter major threats against the Alliance; to ensure European participation in the NATO collective deterrent; and to maintain US involvement in Europe.

During the Cold War, nuclear weapons in Europe had a primarily strategic function (to deter the Soviet Union), while outside Europe they were political tools signifying great-power status. Today, this strategic function is both less important, and increasingly directed towards the WMD threat elsewhere. At the same time, the political function of nuclear weapons is becoming predominant on the continent. Nuclear weapons have a future in Europe because they remain multifaceted policy instruments. They help in achieving security goals, but also support political ones. However, the many reasons advanced to support the continued relevance of nuclear weapons in Europe partly contradict each other, creating new dilemmas.

The first dilemma is related to enlarging institutions and defining a new relationship with Russia. On the one hand, devising a new security relationship with Moscow implies a relative down-grading of nuclear deterrence, as witnessed by NATO's attempts to persuade Russia that there would be no nuclear deployments on the territory of new members. On the other hand, since preserving Alliance solidarity is all the more important as NATO grows, there is a need to maintain the ultimate guarantee embedded in Article 5 of the Washington Treaty, including its implicit nuclear dimension.

The second dilemma concerns the consequences of the slowly emerging European defence and security identity. Could the nuclear dimension be excluded from European integration? If it was, it could be argued that integration would be incomplete given that the ultimate guarantee of Europe's security was left out of the process. But if it was included, there may be a risk of duplication with NATO arrangements similar to that which emerged in the conventional field in the early 1990s. The nuclear element epitomises the whole European defence debate. If the old Atlantic Alliance was about 'keeping the US in, the Russians out and the Germans down', as NATO Secretary-General Lord Ismay once put it, can the new Alliance live with the US half-out, the Russians half-in and the Germans half-up?

the US half-out, the Russians half-in and the Germans half-up

The third dilemma concerns the role of nuclear weapons in deterring WMD proliferation. Reconciling deterrence, which emphasises nuclear weapons, with non-proliferation goals, which necessitate the opposite, could become one of the most fundamental dilemmas of post-Cold War strategy for Western countries.

Possible Outcomes

Several outcomes unfavourable to nuclear deterrence can be envisaged. The first would be a 'transatlantic drift/rift', including a severe crisis in NATO due, for example, to unilateral US moves such as withdrawing nuclear weapons from Europe or adopting a no-first-use doctrine. Other possible developments would concern the value of the US guarantee to Europe. NATO enlargement to encompass Eastern Europe may prompt divisive political debate, for instance in the US Congress, or the US could decide to give priority to its strategic relationship with Russia in the context of START III and follow-on negotiations. Under these circumstances, the US could be tempted to trade 'scope for space' by devaluing the Alliance in return for Russian acquiescence in its expansion. The development of missile-defence systems could also devalue nuclear deterrence.

Overtly downgrading the nuclear dimension of Article 5 of the Washington Treaty would damage Alliance cohesion since Europeans would be unlikely to follow suit. Many would agree with French expert and former IISS Director François Heisbourg that 'the particular advantage the United States has in the conventional [field] should not be allowed to prompt Americans into promoting the view that nuclear weapons are illegitimate'.[1] A future US move towards a 'pure no-first-use' policy (the idea that the sole utility of nuclear weapons is to deter nuclear use) could place severe strain on the Alliance. Some would welcome it, but France, the UK and other European countries would be opposed. Despite Foreign Minister Fischer's statements in 1998, the issue would be likely to prompt heated debate in Germany. In 1992, prominent German experts Thomas Ender, Holger Mey and Michel Rühle warned that 'a US no-first-use declaration would politically invalidate extended deterrence almost entirely'.[2] Some would argue that the first-use option could be kept open in a NATO context, but it is difficult to see how the US could credibly sustain such doctrinal schizophrenia. One side-effect of a US no-first-use pledge could be to encourage Europeans to look more favourably on increased nuclear solidarity among themselves. During the Cold War, the prospect of swift nuclear disarmament raised by the 1986 Reykjavik Summit prompted then British Prime Minister Thatcher to seek nuclear *rapprochement* with France. However, it is by no means clear that building a European deterrent over the remnants of transatlantic solidarity would result in a net security gain.

A second outcome of withdrawing the US nuclear guarantee might be renewed nuclear proliferation in Europe.[3] This is, however, unlikely given the absence of a major threat, the progress in European integration and the readiness of European nuclear powers to play a larger role in EU security. The temptation for non-nuclear states to acquire nuclear weapons would be felt only if three circumstances arose simultaneously: serious threats to European security emerged; extended deterrence disappeared; and a major crisis took place in the European integration process.[4] Possible nuclear-weapon candidates include Germany, Italy, Poland and Turkey. Turkey is a specific case because it has been excluded from the mainstream of European integration. If US nuclear protection significantly eroded, and Turkey felt increasingly left out of new European security arrangements, Ankara could seriously consider developing nuclear weapons, not least given the proliferation threat in the Middle East.[5]

Under a third scenario, nuclear deterrence could decay or 'fade away', leading to a *de facto* 'denuclearisation' of Western strategy in the first decades of the twenty-first century. This could possibly stem from continued international and continental stability, further pressure in favour of disarmament, a 'de-emphasis' of nuclear deterrence and the delegitimisation of nuclear weapons. With the accession to power of social-democratic-oriented political parties in many European states, notably in Germany, it is conceivable that European countries could band together in a concerted effort to reduce the emphasis on nuclear deterrence in the Alliance.

In a more positive outcome for supporters of nuclear deterrence, the Alliance succeeds in managing its looming dilemmas. France's reconciliation to NATO's integrated structure, British moves towards the EU and the emergence of a European defence identity allow for the gradual development of a European nuclear identity within the Alliance. At least in the medium term, this would coexist with NATO's collective deterrent. NATO and Russia would cooperate against the WMD threat, and nuclear deterrence would be acknowledged to play a role in this area in extreme circumstances. The arms-control process would continue in Europe, while all five recognised nuclear powers would engage in talks on stability and alert levels and the feasibility of expanding bilateral treaties such as the ABM and the INF into multilateral arrangements. Later, the UK and France might participate in 'post-START IV' negotiations, after the US and Russia had reached a symbolic level of about 1,000 warheads each.

Barring the emergence of a serious threat to the Alliance, the most probable outcome in the short term is strategic inertia, under which conservatism and a fragile, muted consensus prevail. Most national interests tend in this direction. The US has an interest in leaving current nuclear arrangements untouched. Many in Europe realise that significant changes in Alliance nuclear arrangements would create unmanageable problems. Eastern European countries, which will become key political players, want to be seen as responsible new members of NATO. Governments in France and the UK will want to appear conservative on defence issues, while public interest is less likely to focus on nuclear debates in the absence of new, visible nuclear programmes or deployments. Only the Nordic countries are willing to embark immediately on radical changes, but their political weight in Europe is limited.

This inertia may not, however, last. As demonstrated by the early no-first-use debate, pressures created by new dilemmas and challenges posed by the nuclear question will force governments to take a position one way or the other, and publicly discuss major deterrence issues. Moreover, inertia could be dangerous: nuclear apathy could easily lead to slow but inexorable denuclearisation, leaving the Alliance vulnerable to 'moves made by other actors seeking to capitalize on the reluctance of many allied officials to address nuclear issues'.[6] Worse, the Allies could be unprepared for the next crisis with a WMD/nuclear dimension. Under these circumstances, it is important to ensure that nuclear policies are adjusted without derailing the nuclear and European security debates.

Desirable Strategies

The US would be wise to adopt a prudent, conservative attitude towards Alliance nuclear policy. It would be sensible to reaffirm the value of Article 5 in the context of enlargement, and avoid any sharp shift towards an overt no-first-use policy. NATO would find it useful to consider adopting a doctrine based on 'no-first-use of WMD'. A carefully crafted declaratory policy would confirm the Allies' resolve to deter aggression by whatever means, not just nuclear threats. It should also underline that the primary, although not exclusive, utility of nuclear weapons lies in deterring threats against national territories. NATO could then reduce the emphasis on nuclear first-use against a conventional threat in Europe, while at the same time emphasising the value of deterrence against WMD use in a regional context. NATO might also, to the extent possible, increase the number and frequency of exercises and war-games with a nuclear-deterrence dimension so as to maintain the 'nuclear culture' on the continent. US B-61 gravity bombs should remain in Europe. The idea, floated in Alliance circles, of consolidating the NATO deterrent into a single dual-capable-aircraft wing at one site should be handled with care since it could reduce risk- and responsibility-sharing to the point where many would consider that the B-61s might as well be withdrawn altogether. Host countries could be encouraged to maintain their financial contribution to the collective deterrent, including, perhaps, through a special fund to which all NATO members contribute. Failing to sustain these financial commitments could encourage those who wish to reduce or end permanent US nuclear deployments in Europe.

Alliance states would be wise to foster carefully the perception that new members are covered by the same nuclear guarantees as 'Cold War' ones. If the nuclear protection of Western Europe were downplayed, it is likely that everyone would lose because the net effect would be a perceived degradation of the US guarantee as a whole. Trading scope for space with Russia should not be an option; instead, the Nordic model (voluntary renunciation of nuclear weapons on national territory) should be applied to Central and Eastern Europeans. At the same time, the possibility of deploying weapons in the East in a crisis should not at this point be foreclosed, if it proves acceptable by NATO safety, security and efficiency standards without having to build dedicated infrastructure such as storage vaults.

In deference to Russia's position as a nuclear-weapon state, a 'nuclear special relationship' with Moscow could be developed, expanding on the provisions of the 1997 Founding Act. This could at some point include joint political–military war-games and exercises involving regional WMD threats. Other options for enhancing strategic stability include negotiating measures on transparency and alert levels. The Alliance needs to avoid presenting its nuclear weapons stationed in Europe as the mirror-image of, or counter-weight to, Russian tactical/theatre nuclear weapons, since doing so would risk making them vulnerable to a Russian diplomatic offensive for a total ban. But NATO countries could invite Russia to explore joint efforts to foster tactical/theatre nuclear arms control. Proposals by Sweden and Norway in 1996 to codify the 1991 unilateral US and Soviet commitments to withdraw and retire most of their theatre nuclear weapons deserve serious examination, although achieving a verifiable arms-control agreement would be a significant challenge. A formal arrangement banning the permanent deployment of nuclear weapons in Central and Eastern Europe could be considered. Although NATO policy has sought to gain the advantages of a *de facto* nuclear-weapon-free zone without the inconveniences of a *de jure* one, such a zone could be envisaged in the longer term – if, on balance, Eastern European countries considered that it would increase their security, and if it included the Kaliningrad enclave. A nuclear-weapon-free zone would have some important benefits. It could reassure Russia as to NATO enlargement and would prevent Moscow from deploying weapons in Belarus or Kaliningrad. It would also be seen as positive in terms of Western implementation of Article VI of the NPT. Other proposals, such as a total ban on nuclear deployments outside national territories, put forward by Russia, China and some NGOs, should continue to be firmly rejected.

In line with a policy based on 'no-first-use of WMD', it could perhaps be time to suggest a bilateral no-first-use agreement with Russia given the disappearance of the massive conventional threat in Europe. This could be made conditional on the full and continued implementation of the Conventional Armed Forces in Europe (CFE) Treaty. Since Russia is as dependent on nuclear weapons as the Alliance was during the Cold War, Moscow is unlikely to view this proposal favourably. Nonetheless, the proposal could have confidence-building value and, given that it could be reversed in as much time as it takes to retarget a detargeted missile, would do little to compromise deterrence *vis-à-vis* any future resurgent Russia. In the unlikely event that Russia again became a conventional threat, nothing would preclude readjusting Alliance policy accordingly. Mechanisms for a specific European contribution to dismantling Russia's tactical/theatre arsenal could be devised, perhaps taking the form of a 'European Cooperative Threat Reduction' programme. (A division of labour, where the US takes care of 'strategic' weapons and the Europeans manage the rest, would be artificial and politically inappropriate.)[7] Finally, exchanges of views on nuclear deterrence with the other PfP states could be considered.

Alliance debates on nuclear issues should give a wider role to Europeans, including to smaller nations. Europe should be given additional responsibilities in preparing nuclear-policy decisions, and rotation should involve the maximum number of European countries so that military and political staffs are familiarised with nuclear issues and procedures. The HLG and DGP could be merged, with US–European co-chairmanship. In the longer term, the WEU could nominate an officer formally to represent Europe at STRATCOM. Although measures such as these could seem tantamount to a net reduction of US power and influence in the Alliance, they would help to maintain the transatlantic nuclear consensus and bolster European support for NATO. They would thus benefit the US.

Europeans need to play a larger part in nuclear-doctrine debates

After monetary union is completed, and assuming that the UK joins, European countries willing to do so should embark on an in-depth dialogue encompassing all military nuclear issues. In all likelihood, only 'core' European countries such as France, Germany, the UK, the Benelux states, Italy and Spain would be willing to participate. Initially, this would not pose a problem; only if a European deterrent were to develop in the longer term would it be desirable to find a way to avoid 'free-riding on a collective good', as, for instance, Sweden apparently did during the Cold War.[8] To boost this process, France and the UK could declare publicly that their nuclear forces protect the EU's vital interests. Europe could then gradually develop its own nuclear identity on an *ad hoc* basis, not as an instrument of prestige or 'grandeur', but as one of international stability and strategic autonomy. This process needs to be transparent for other nations concerned, notably the US, but also Norway and Turkey. Multilateral discussions in Alliance and European *ad hoc* fora therefore should not be insulated from each other.

Maintaining Alliance nuclear consensus will be at least as difficult in the new strategic environment as it was in the old. The dilemmas facing NATO correspond to cultural differences between the US and Europe. There are other potential faultlines – divergences between nuclear and non-nuclear powers over the role of nuclear deterrence in relation to WMD proliferation, or among nuclear powers over the importance of a European dimension to deterrence. But transatlantic divergence seems potentially the most significant. In particular, it is doubtful whether European countries will follow the US in downgrading the importance of nuclear weapons in world security and Alliance matters. Barring the emergence of a direct military threat against Europe or, worse, the actual use of a nuclear weapon somewhere in the world, the most important engines of change in nuclear deterrence in Europe remain internal to the Alliance, and lie largely in the hands of NATO's three nuclear powers. The coming debates could make or break the nuclear consensus within the Alliance, and Europe's political leaders will need to proceed with caution. The multiplicity of rationales put forward in support of the continued relevance of nuclear weapons in post-Cold War Europe may create confusion. Nuclear weapons in Europe may face being 'overlegitimised', rather than 'delegitimised'. Whichever policies are chosen, public support for new options might be difficult to gain. A delicate balance will have to be struck between the need to tackle issues which are fundamental to the future of European security, and the risk of reopening old wounds.

notes

Acknowledgments

The author would like to thank Pascal Boniface, Olivier Debouzy, Thérèse Delpech, François Heisbourg, Robert Irvine, Burkard Schmitt and David S. Yost for their comments on an earlier draft of this paper.

Introduction

[1] During the Cold War, some 13,000 NATO and Soviet nuclear weapons, from low-yield artillery shells and atomic demolition munitions to powerful medium-range ballistic missiles (MRBMs), were permanently stationed in Europe.
[2] 'Final Communiqué issued at the Ministerial Meeting of the North Atlantic Council', Press Communiqué M-NAC-2 (96)165, 10 December 1996, paragraph 5.
[3] Michael Quinlan, *Thinking about Nuclear Weapons*, Whitehall Paper 41 (London: Royal United Services Institute (RUSI), 1997).
[4] See IISS, 'Nuclear Weapons First

in Russia's Defence Policy', *Strategic Comments*, vol. 4, no. 1, January 1998.

Chapter 1

[1] *Summary Report of the Allied–Central European Workshop on Post-Cold War Concepts of Deterrence* (Cambridge, MA: Institute for Foreign Policy Analysis/National Security Planning Associates, 1996).
[2] *Ibid*.
[3] See *United States Security Strategy for Europe and NATO* (Washington DC: Department of Defense (DoD), June 1995), p. 32.
[4] 'Final Communiqué of the Ministerial Meetings of the Defence Planning Committee and the Nuclear Planning Group', Press Communiqué M-DPC/NPG-2(96)173, 17 December 1996, paragraph 7; 'Nuclear Notebook: Where the Bombs Are, 1997', *Bulletin of the Atomic Scientists*, September 1997, p. 62; and *Nuclear*

Weapons and the European Defence Identity, Working Document, Political Series W-22 (Luxembourg: European Parliament Directorate-General for Research, October 1996), p. 20. Tentative assessments of the US nuclear presence and European nuclear roles include William M. Arkin, Robert S. Norris and Joshua Handler, *Taking Stock: Worldwide Nuclear Deployments 1998* (Washington DC: Natural Resources Defense Council, 1998); and Martin Butcher, Otfried Nassauer and Stephen Young, *Nuclear Futures: Western European Options for Nuclear Risk Reductions*, BASIC/BITS Research Report 98.6 (London: British–American Security Council, 1998).

[5] 'NATO's Nuclear Forces in the New Security Environment', *NATO Fact Sheet*, November 1997.

[6] Stanley R. Sloan, *NATO Nuclear Strategy: Issues for US Policy*, CRS Report for Congress 96-653-F (Washington DC: Congressional Research Service (CRS), 25 July 1996), p. 10.

[7] *NATO Nuclear Bases: US Should Seek Needs Reassessment and Increased Alliance Contributions* (Washington DC: US General Accounting Office (GAO), 1993), p. 2.

[8] Andrew G. B. Wallace, 'New Thinking about the Unthinkable?', unpublished paper, October 1996.

[9] 'Final Communiqué of the Ministerial Meetings of the Defence Planning Committee and the Nuclear Planning Group', Press Communiqué M-DPC/NPG-1(95)57, 8 June 1995; and 'Final Communiqué of the Meeting of the Defence Planning Committee in Ministerial Session', Press Communiqué M-DPC/NPG-1(96)88, 13 June 1996.

[10] See Butcher, Nassauer and Young, *Nuclear Futures*.

[11] 'The London Declaration on a Transformed North Atlantic Alliance', Summit of Alliance Heads of State and Government, London, 6 July 1990, paragraph 18.

[12] 'The Alliance's Strategic Concept', Summit of Alliance Heads of State and Government, Rome, 7 November 1991, paragraphs 55 and 56.

[13] *1994 White Paper* (Bonn: Federal Ministry of Defence, 1994), p. 52 (French edition).

[14] 'Final Communiqué', 13 June 1996.

[15] Armed Forces Minister John Reid, *Written Answers to Questions*, UK House of Commons, 20 May 1997.

[16] David Omand, 'Nuclear Deterrence in a Changing World: The View from a UK Perspective', *RUSI Journal*, vol. 141, no. 3, June 1996, p. 19.

[17] 'Founding Act on Mutual Relations, Cooperation and Security between NATO and the Russian Federation', Paris, 27 May 1997.

[18] See Bruno Tertrais, *The French Nuclear Deterrent after the Cold War* (Santa Monica, CA: RAND, 1998).

[19] *Livre Blanc sur la Défense 1994* (Paris: Service d'Information et de Relations Publiques des Armées (SIRPA)/Ministère de la Défense, 1994), p. 52.

[20] *Ibid.*, p. 50.

[21] See François Heisbourg, 'La France et le Désarmement Nucléaire', *La Revue Internationale et Stratégique*, no. 30, Summer 1998, pp. 49–54 ; and Pascal Boniface, *Repenser la Dissuasion Nucléaire* (Paris: Editions de l'Aube, 1997).

[22] Lionel Jospin, speech to the Institut des Hautes Etudes de

Défense Nationale, 4 September 1997. On French nuclear debates, see Tertrais, *The French Nuclear Deterrent*; and Camille Grand, *A French Nuclear Exception?*, Occasional Paper 38 (Washington DC: Henry L. Stimson Center, 1998).

[23] UK Ministry of Defence, 'Nuclear Free-Fall Bombs to be Withdrawn from Service by 1998', Press Release 47/95, 4 April 1995.

[24] Omand, 'Nuclear Deterrence', pp. 15–22.

[25] *Ibid.*, p. 20.

[26] Malcolm Rifkind, 'UK Defence Strategy: A Continuing Role for Nuclear Weapons?', speech to the Centre for Defence Studies, King's College London, 16 November 1993.

[27] Omand, 'Nuclear Deterrence'.

[28] *A Fresh Start for Britain: Labour's Strategy for Britain in the Modern World* (London: The Labour Party, 1996).

[29] David Henderson, 'Shaping the UK's Minimum Deterrent for the Turn of the Century', *RUSI Journal*, vol. 140, no. 3, June 1995.

[30] Reid, *Written Answers*.

[31] See Paul Rogers, *Substrategic Trident: A Slow Burning Fuse*, London Defence Studies 34 (London: Brassey's for the Centre for Defence Studies, April 1996); and Rebecca Johnson, *British Perspectives on the Future of Nuclear Weapons*, Occasional Paper 37 (Washington DC: Henry L. Stimson Center, 1998).

[32] *NATO Nuclear Bases*, p. 4.

[33] Sloan, *NATO Nuclear Strategy*, p. 1.

[34] *Nuclear Weapons and the European Defence Identity*, p. 20; Christopher Bellamy, 'UK: Wind of Change as US Removes Last Nuclear Bombs from Britain', *The Independent*, 28 October 1996.

[35] Giuseppe Cucchi, 'La Difesa Nucleare Europea e la "Dissuasion Concertée"', *Affari Esteri*, January 1997, p. 718.

[36] Federal Ministry of Defence, *1994 White Paper*, p. 52.

[37] 'No Arsenis Comment on Nuclear Weapon Charge', in Foreign Broadcast Information Service (FBIS), *Daily Report*, WEU-95-074, 18 April 1995; 'Weapons Presence Acknowledged', *ibid.*, WEU-96-077, 19 April 1995.

Chapter 2

[1] See David S. Yost, 'The Delegitimization of Nuclear Deterrence?', *Armed Forces and Society*, vol. 16, no. 4, Summer 1990, pp. 487–508.

[2] On European public opinion during the Cold War, see Stephen F. Szabo, 'Public Opinion and the Atlantic Alliance', in Stanley R. Sloan (ed.), *NATO in the 1990s* (London: Pergamon-Brassey's for the North Atlantic Assembly, 1989), pp. 143–72.

[3] See 'Nuclear Weapons: The Abolitionist Upsurge', *Strategic Survey 1997/98* (Oxford: Oxford University Press for the IISS, 1998), pp. 45–54.

[4] See, for example, Hans M. Kristensen and Joshua Handler, *The 520 Forgotten Bombs: How US and British Nuclear Weapons in Europe Undermine the Non-Proliferation Treaty* (Washington DC: Greenpeace International, October 1995); and 'Joint Statement by the Ministers for Foreign Affairs of Brazil, Egypt, Ireland, Mexico, New Zealand, Slovenia, South Africa and Sweden', 9 June 1998.

[5] See Freimut Duve, 'Le Nucléaire

n'est plus l'Instrument de la Dissuasion', *Le Monde*, 24 August 1995, p. 11.

[6] Rudolf Scharping, 'Lizenzkriege? Ohne Deutsche!', *Die Zeit*, 2 September 1993.

[7] See Ronald D. Asmus, *Germany in Transition: National Self-Confidence and International Reticence* (Santa Monica, CA: RAND, 1992).

[8] For an overview, see Richard Sinnott, *Opinion Publique et Politique Sécuritaire de l'Europe*, Cahiers de Chaillot 28 (Paris: Western European Union (WEU) Institute for Security Studies, 1997).

[9] According to a European Commission poll in 1993, in Belgium, France, Germany, Italy the Netherlands and the UK, less than 50% show 'aversion to the nuclear risk'; in Denmark, Greece, Ireland and Portugal, the rate is above this threshold. See Jean-Pierre Pagès, 'L'Opinion Européenne et les Questions Energétiques en 1993', *Eurobarometer 1993* (Brussels: European Commission, 1993).

[10] Andrew F. Krepinevich and Stephen M. Kosiak, 'Smarter Bombs, Fewer Nukes', *Bulletin of the Atomic Scientists*, November–December 1998, pp. 26–32.

[11] Interview with unnamed State Department official in Mark Hibbs, 'Tomorrow, a Eurobomb?', *ibid.*, January–February 1996, p. 19.

[12] See *NATO Nuclear Bases*.

[13] See IISS, 'The US No-First-Use Debate', *Strategic Comments*, vol. 2, no. 9, November 1996.

[14] Les Aspin, 'From Deterrence to Denuking: Dealing with Proliferation in the 1990s', in *Shaping Nuclear Policy in the 1990s: A Compendium of Views* (Washington DC: House Armed Services Committee, 1992).

[15] Sloan, *NATO Nuclear Strategy*, p. 11.

[16] National Academy of Sciences, Committee on International Security and Arms Control, *The Future of US Nuclear Weapons Policy* (Washington DC: National Academy Press, 1997), p. 39.

[17] Stephen P. Lambert and David A. Miller, *Russia's Crumbling Tactical Nuclear Weapons Complex: An Opportunity for Arms Control*, INSS Occasional Paper 12 (Colorado Springs, CO: Institute for National Security Studies, April 1997), pp. 32–33.

[18] Andrew J. Goodpaster *et al.*, *Nuclear Weapons and European Security* (Washington DC: Atlantic Council of the United States, April 1996).

[19] National Academy of Sciences, *The Future of US Nuclear Weapons Policy*, p. 72.

[20] Goodpaster Committee, 'Nuclear Roles in the Post-Cold War World', *Washington Quarterly*, vol. 20, no. 3, Summer 1997, pp. 163–66.

[21] 'Confusion about NATO', *New York Times*, 8 December 1998.

[22] 'British–French Statement on European Defence, Saint-Malo, 4 December 1998'.

[23] See Christoph Bluth, *Britain, Germany and Western Nuclear Strategy*, Nuclear History Programme 3 (Oxford: Clarendon Press, 1995).

[24] On post-Cold War Anglo-French nuclear cooperation, see Stuart Croft, 'European Integration, Nuclear Deterrence and French–British Nuclear Cooperation', *International Affairs*, vol. 72, no. 4, October 1996, pp. 771–87.

[25] See Olivier Debouzy, *Anglo-French Nuclear Cooperation: Perspectives and Problems*, Whitehall Paper 7 (London: RUSI, 1991).

[26] Statement by John Major, press conference closing the Franco-British Summit, London, 26 July 1993.

[27] Rifkind, 'UK Defence Strategy'.

[28] 'UK–French Joint Statement on Nuclear Cooperation', 30 October 1995.

[29] Rob de Wijk, *NATO on the Brink of the New Millennium: The Battle for Consensus*, Atlantic Commentaries Series (London: Brassey's, 1997), pp. 38–39.

Chapter 3

[1] Comment by UK Secretary of State for Defence Rifkind at the symposium 'Elargir la Dissuasion?', Paris, 30 September 1992.

[2] 'General Eugene Habiger, Commander-in-Chief, US Strategic Command', interview by Jeff Erlich, *Defense News*, 10–16 March 1997, p. 70.

[3] Friedbert Pflüger quoted in Hibbs, 'Tomorrow, a Eurobomb?', p. 22.

[4] Duygu Bazoglu Sezer, 'Turkey's New Security Environment, Nuclear Weapons and Proliferation', *Comparative Strategy*, vol. 14, no. 2, 1995, pp. 149–72.

[5] 'President Says Nuclear Weapons Deployment up to NATO', *BBC Summary of World Broadcasts Central Europe* (SWB/EE) D2879/C, 28 March 1997.

[6] Jacques Chirac, 'Prolifération, Non-Prolifération, Dissuasion', *Politique Internationale*, no. 56, Summer 1992, pp. 9–34.

[7] Jacques Chirac, speech at the meeting of French ambassadors, Paris, 31 August 1995.

[8] 'Communication du Ministre des Affaires Etrangères M. Alain Juppé à la Commission des Affaires Etrangères, de la Défense et des Forces Armées du Sénat', in *Politique Etrangère de la France* (Paris: Le Documentation Française, March–April 1995), p. 157.

[9] *Ibid.*, p. 4.

[10] Jospin, speech to the Institut des Hautes Etudes de Défense Nationale, 4 September 1997.

[11] Lawrence Freedman, *The Revolution in Strategic Affairs*, Adelphi Paper 318 (Oxford: Oxford University Press for the IISS, 1998), p. 47.

[12] Comment by Rifkind at the symposium 'Elargir la Dissuasion', 30 September 1992.

[13] Rifkind, 'UK Defence Strategy'.

[14] *Ibid.*

[15] Omand, 'Nuclear Deterrence', pp. 15–22.

[16] *The UK Strategic Defence Review* (London: The Stationery Office, 1998), p. 16.

[17] Armed Forces Minister Reid quoted in Butcher, Nassauer and Young, *Nuclear Futures*.

[18] Lord Hoyle, *Written Answers to Questions*, UK House of Lords, 29 October 1998.

[19] See Ashton B. Carter and David B. Omand, 'Countering the Proliferation Risk: Adapting the Alliance to the New Security Environment', *NATO Review*, vol. 44, no. 5, September 1996, pp. 10–15; and Gregory L. Schulte, 'Responding to Proliferation – NATO's Role', *ibid.*, vol. 43, no. 4, July 1995, pp. 15–19.

[20] Omand, 'Nuclear Deterrence', p. 19.

[21] 'NATO's Nuclear Forces in the New Security Environment'.

[22] See, for example, Claudio Virgi, 'Armi Batteriologiche, Come Difendersi?', *Il Sole 24 Ore*, 30

September 1995. For a comprehensive treatment of Turkey and weapons of mass destruction (WMD), see Mustafa Kibaroglu, 'Turkey', in Harald Müller (ed.), *Europe and Nuclear Disarmament: Debates and Political Attitudes in 16 European Countries* (Brussels: European Interuniversity Press/Frankfurt Peace Research Institute, 1998), pp. 161–93.

[23] Volker Rühe quoted in Michael Evans, 'NATO Says Farewell to Nuclear Conflict', *The Times*, 21 October 1992.

[24] On this issue, see Karl-Heinz Kamp, 'Maintain First-Use Policy', *Defense News*, 7–13 December 1998, p. 29; Harald Müller, Alexander Kelle, Katja Frank, Sylvia Meier and Annette Schaper, 'The German Debate on Nuclear Weapons and Disarmament', *Washington Quarterly*, vol. 20, no. 3, Summer 1997, pp. 115–22; and Uwe Nerlich, *Nuclear Forces and Coalition Strategy in the Decades Ahead*, Futures Roles Series Paper 6 (Albuquerque, NM: Sandia National Laboratories, August 1996).

[25] McGeorge Bundy, George F. Kennan, Robert S. McNamara and Gerald Smith, 'Nuclear Weapons and the Atlantic Alliance', *Foreign Affairs*, vol. 60, no. 4, Spring 1982, pp. 753–68.

[26] Karl Kaiser, Georg Leber, Alois Mertes and Franz-Josef Schultze, 'Nuclear Weapons and the Preservation of Peace', *Foreign Affairs*, vol. 60, no. 5, Summer 1982, pp. 1,157–70.

[27] Robert O'Neill, 'Britain and the Future of Nuclear Weapons', *International Affairs*, vol. 71, no. 4, October 1995, pp. 747–61.

[28] André Dumoulin, 'L'OTAN, l'UEO et le Lien Transatlantique: l'Avenir de la Dissuasion Nucléaire en Europe', *Veiligheid en Strategie*, no. 48, June 1996, pp. 97–147.

[29] Roberto Zadra, *L'Intégration Européenne et la Dissuasion Nucléaire après la Guerre Froide*, Cahiers de Chaillot 5 (Paris: WEU Institute for Security Studies, November 1992), p. 19.

[30] See 'Paris Réaffirme Son Attachement à la Dissuasion Nucléaire', *Agence-France Presse*, 25 November 1998; and UK Secretary of Defence George Robertson, *Written Answers to Questions*, House of Commons, 2 December 1998.

[31] Stefan Kornelius and Christoph Schwennicke, 'Minister für Selbstverteidigung', *Süddeutsche Zeitung*, 25 November 1998.

[32] Harald Müller, 'L'Union Européenne et la Dissuasion Nucléaire: Evaluation Critique', *Relations Internationales et Stratégiques*, no. 21, Spring 1996, p. 110.

[33] Omand, 'Nuclear Deterrence in a Changing World', p. 21.

[34] Nicholas K. J. Witney, 'British Nuclear Policy after the Cold War', *Survival*, vol. 36, no. 4, Winter 1994–95, pp. 101–102.

[35] Quinlan, *Thinking about Nuclear Weapons*, p. 51.

[36] Rifkind, 'UK Defence Strategy'.

[37] See Müller (ed.), *Europe and Nuclear Disarmament*, p. 29.

[38] *Atlantic News*, no. 3,065, 10 December 1998.

[39] David Gompert, Kenneth Watman and Dean Wilkening, 'Nuclear First Use Revisited', *Survival*, vol. 37, no. 3, Autumn 1995, pp. 27–44. For European reactions, see Michael Quinlan, 'Letter to the Editor', *ibid.*, vol. 37, no. 4, Winter 1995–96, pp. 189–91; Martyn Piper and Bruno Tertrais, *Deterrence, Weapons of Mass Destruction and Security Assurances*

(Santa Monica, CA: RAND, 1996); and Stephen Pullinger, *Preventing the Use of Chemical and Biological Weapons: Implications for Negative Security Assurances*, ISIS Briefing 72 (London: International Security Information Service, July 1998).

[40] Kamp, 'Maintain First-Use Policy'.

[41] *NATO Nuclear Bases*, p. 4.

[42] *Ibid.*, p. 5.

[43] See Stephen P. Lambert and David A. Miller, *US Nuclear Weapons in Europe: The Current Environment and Prospects for the Future*, Thesis (Monterey, CA: Naval Postgraduate School, December 1996), p. 108.

[44] As Jacquelyn Davis, Charles Perry and Andrew Winner of the US Institute for Foreign Policy Analysis put it in 1997: 'whereas a nuclear strike from an aircraft would probably require a substantial "support package", off-shore systems are capable of "going it alone"'. See Davis, Perry and Winner, 'The Looming Alliance Debate Over Nuclear Weapons', *Joint Force Quarterly*, no. 17, Spring 1997, p. 111.

[45] Karl Kaiser, 'From Nuclear Deterrence to Graduated Conflict Control', *Survival*, vol. 32, no. 6, November 1990, pp. 483–96.

[46] Mark N. Gose, 'The New Germany and Nuclear Weapons: Options for the Future', *Airpower Journal*, Special Edition, vol. 10, 1996, p. 78; Walter B. Slocombe, 'The Future of US Nuclear Weapons in a Restructured World', in Patrick J. Garrity and Steven A. Maaranen (eds), *Nuclear Weapons in the Changing World: Perspectives from Europe, Asia and North America* (New York: Plenum, 1992), p. 63.

[47] Stansfield Turner, *Caging the Nuclear Genie: An American Challenge for Global Security* (Boulder, CO: Westview Press, 1997), p. 77.

[48] Michael J. Mazaar and Alexander T. Lennon (eds), *Toward a Nuclear Peace* (New York: St Martin's Press, 1994), pp. 48–49.

[49] Karl-Heinz Kamp, 'Germany and the Future of Nuclear Weapons in Europe', in Thomas-Durrell Young (ed.), *Force Statecraft and German Unity: The Struggle to Adapt Institutions and Practices* (Carlisle, PA: Strategic Studies Institute, December 1996), pp. 27–48.

[50] Davis, Perry and Winner, 'The Looming Alliance Debate', p. 113.

[51] Harald Müller and Kalja Frank, 'A German View of Nuclear Postures', *Policy Brief*, vol. 1, no. 15, October 1997.

[52] *Nuclear Weapons and the European Defence Identity*, p. 20.

[53] On this point, see Suzanne Peters, *The Germans and the INF Missiles* (Baden-Baden: Nomos Politik, 1990); and Karl-Heinz Kamp, 'Die Nuklearen Kurzstreckenwaffen der NATO 1945–1991', *Strategie und Politik* (Sankt Augustin: Konrad-Adenauer-Stiftung, 1993).

[54] Davis, Perry and Winner, 'The Looming Alliance Debate', p. 85.

[55] Lawrence Freedman, *Does Deterrence Have a Future?*, Future Roles Series Paper 5 (Albuquerque, NM: Sandia National Laboratories, June 1996), p. 20.

[56] Davis, Perry and Winner, 'The Looming Alliance Debate', p. 83.

[57] Catherine McArdle Kelleher and Kenneth Myers Sr., 'Nuclear Deterrence and European Security', in Hans Binnendijk and James Goodby (eds), *Transforming Nuclear Deterrence* (Washington DC: National Defense University (NDU) Press, 1997).

58 David S. Broder, 'Brave New NATO', *Washington Post*, 22 April 1998, p. A23.

59 Fareed Zakaria, 'Can Russia Join the Club, Too?', *Newsweek*, 4 May 1998, p. 44, cited by Senator Patrick Moynihan, Senate Armed Services Committee Hearings, 27 April 1998. This argument has been raised by a variety of authors. See Sloan, *NATO Nuclear Strategy*, p. 13 ; Thomas L. Friedman, 'Iraq is Bad, but the Biggest Proliferation Threat is Russia', *International Herald Tribune*, 18 February 1998, p. 8; Susan Eisenhower, 'NATO Expansion: Just Say No', *Armed Forces Journal International*, March 1998, p. 47; and Jack Mendelssohn, 'NATO Expansion: A Decision to Regret', *Arms Control Today*, June–July 1997, p. 2.

60 See Stephen J. Cimbala, 'Russia and Nuclear Coercion: How Necessary? How Much?', *Journal of Slavic Military Studies*, vol. 10, no. 3, September 1997, pp. 56–78.

61 *Study on NATO Enlargement* (Brussels: NATO, September 1995), paragraphs 45d and 58.

62 'Founding Act on Mutual Relations, Cooperation and Security between NATO and the Russian Federation', Paris, 27 May 1997.

63 'Foreign Minister Rejects Russian Idea of Neutrality', in SWB/EE D2880/C, 31 March 1997.

64 Polish President Alexander Kwasniewski, quoted in Bruce Clark, 'Kwasniewski Gives NATO Assurance', *Financial Times*, 25 October 1996; and Defence Minister Stanislaw Dobrzanski, quoted in Sabine Verhest, 'Varsovie Met le Cap sur l'Alliance Atlantique', *Libre Belgique*, 15 April 1997.

65 *Summary Report of the Allied–Central European Workshop*, p. II; 'Half of Slovaks Support NATO Membership – Poll', SWB/EE D2897/C, 19 April 1997.

66 See Francesco Calogero, 'A Nuclear-Weapon-Free Zone in Central and Eastern Europe', *Pugwash Newsletter*, May 1997, pp. 67–70; Jan Prawitz, 'A Nuclear-Weapon-Free Zone in Central and Eastern Europe', Programme for Promoting Nuclear Non-Proliferation, *Issue Review*, no. 10, February 1997; and *The Future of US Nuclear Weapons Policy*, pp. 69–70.

67 See Belgian Foreign Affairs Minister Erik Derycke, 'Un Elargissement de l'Otan sur une Base Consensuelle est Possible et Souhaitable', *Le Soir*, 15 January 1997.

68 William S. Cohen, testimony before the Senate Armed Services Committee, *USIS Washington File*, 23 April 1997.

69 Article 5.3 of the Two Plus Four Treaty states that 'armed forces and nuclear weapons or foreign nuclear launchers will not be stationed and will not be deployed on [the territory of the current German Democratic Republic]'. However, an 'agreed minute to the treaty' states that 'any question regarding the implementation of the word "deployed" … will be solved by the Government of the united Germany in a responsible and reasonable way, taking into account the security interests of each contracting Party'.

70 'Foreign Minister Says NATO Enlargement Row with Russia Over', SWB/EE D/2922/C, 19 May 1997.

71 Lionel Jospin, speech to the Institut des Hautes Etudes de Défense Nationale, 3 September

1998.

[72] *UK Strategic Defence Review*, p. 19.

[73] Comment by Defence Minister Alain Richard, 'La France et l'Arme Nucléaire', Roundtable, Paris, 27 August 1998.

Chapter 4

[1] 'Platform on European Security Interests', The Hague, 27 October 1987.

[2] On this issue, see Marie-Hélène Labbé, 'Y a-t-il une Politique Européenne de Non-Prolifération Nucléaire?', *Politique Etrangère*, vol. 62, no. 3, Autumn 1997, pp. 307–19.

[3] François Mitterrand, quoted in Jacques Amalric, 'La Construction Communautaire et l'Avenir de la Force de Dissuasion', *Le Monde*, 13 January 1992.

[4] 'M. Mellick Recense les Différentes Formules d'une Doctrine Nucléaire Européenne', *Le Monde*, 4 February 1992.

[5] Alain Juppé, speech to the Institut des Hautes Etudes de Défense Nationale, Paris, 7 September 1995.

[6] 'Annexe à la Loi No. 96-589 du 2 Juillet 1996 Relative à la Programmation Militaire pour les Années 1997 à 2002', *Journal Officiel de la République Française*, 3 July 1996, p. 9,988.

[7] Hubert Védrine, 'Dissuasion Elargie ou Européenne', *Le Point*, no. 1,202, 30 September 1995.

[8] Pascal Boniface, 'Dissuasion Concertée, Octroyée, Contestée', *Le Monde*, 12 September 1995.

[9] Jospin, speech to the Institut des Hautes Etudes de Défense Nationale, 4 September 1997.

[10] *Livre Blanc sur la Défense* (Paris: Gouvernement de la République Française, 1972), p. 9.

[11] See, for instance, Frédéric Bozo,

'Dissuasion Concertée: Le Sens de la Formule', *Relations Internationales et Stratégiques*, no. 21, Spring 1996, p. 99.

[12] Chirac, speech to the Institut des Hautes Etudes de Défense Nationale, Paris, 8 June 1996.

[13] Alain Juppé, 'Quel Horizon pour la Politique Etrangère de la France?', speech marking the twentieth anniversary of the Policy Planning Staff, Paris, 30 January 1995, reproduced in *Politique Etrangère*, no. 1, 1995, pp. 245–59.

[14] See, for instance, Olivier Debouzy, 'France/OTAN: La Fin de l'autre Guerre Froide', *Commentaire*, no. 74, Summer 1996, pp. 349–52.

[15] Javier Solana, quoted in André Dumoulin, 'Les Aléas de la Dissuasion Concertée', *Libération*, 2 June 1996.

[16] Christopher Mallaby, 'Pourquoi la Grande-Bretagne a Soutenu la France', *Le Figaro*, 14 December 1995.

[17] See 'Bonn Interested in French Nuclear Shield for Germany', *Reuters*, 29 September 1995; Friedbert Pflüger, 'Et si l'Allemagne Acceptait le Parapluie Nucléaire Français?', *Premières Conférences Stratégiques Annuelles de l'IRIS* (Paris: La Documentation Française, 1997), p. 71; and Jean-Paul Picaper, 'Bonn Est Favorable à la Concertation avec Paris', *Le Figaro*, 29 January 1997.

[18] Kamp, 'Reshaping Nuclear Europe', *Defense News*, vol. 12, no. 16, 14 April 1997, p. 19.

[19] See Müller, Kelle, Frank, Meier and Schaper, 'The German Debate on Nuclear Weapons', p. 122; Holger H. Mey and Andrew Denison, 'France's Nuclear Tests and Germany's Nuclear Interests', *Comparative Strategy*, vol. 15, no. 2,

1996, p. 171; and Günther Nonnenmacher, 'Ein Angebot aus Paris', *Frankfurter Allgemeine Zeitung*, 13 September 1995.

[20] See Kamp, 'Germany and the Future of Nuclear Weapons in Europe'; Florian Gerster and Michael Hennes, 'Minimalabschreckung durch die Kernwaffen Englands und Frankreichs', *Europaeische Wehrkunde*, vol. 34, August 1990, p. 443; and Peter Schmidt, *Le Couple Franco-Allemand et la Sécurité dans les Années 90: L'Avenir d'une Relation Privilégiée*, Cahiers de Chaillot 8 (Paris: WEU Institute for Security Studies, June 1993).

[21] See Burkard Schmitt, *L'Europe et la Dissuasion Nucléaire*, Occasional Paper 3 (Paris: WEU Institute for Security Studies, October 1997).

[22] See Duve, 'Le Nucléaire n'est plus l'Instrument de la Dissuasion'; and interview with Alfred Dregger, *Die Welt*, 26 September 1995.

[23] Interview with Volker Rühe, German television channel ARD, 29 January 1997.

[24] See Arnaud Leparmentier, 'Joshka Fischer Plaide pour une "Politique Intérieure Européenne"', *Le Monde*, 28 October 1998.

[25] Volker Rühe, quoted in Lorraine Millot, 'Foudre Allemande sur le Parapluie Français', *Libération*, 15 September 1995.

[26] Mey and Denison, 'France's Nuclear Tests', p. 170.

[27] See Marco Carnovale, 'Why NATO-Europe Needs a Nuclear Trigger', *Orbis*, vol. 35, no. 2, Spring 1991, pp. 223–33; and Zadra, *L'Intégration Européenne*.

[28] For Italian reactions, see Claudio Virgi, 'Il Deterrente Nucleare Francese Garantisce la Difese dell'Europe', *Il Sole 24 Ore*, 16 June 1995; 'L'Europea Integri la Francia Potenza Nucleare', *ibid.*, 24 November 1995; and Cucchi, 'La Difesa Nucleare Europea'.

[29] See Jorge Aspizua Turrion, *Europa? Potencia Nuclear?*, Cuadernos de Estrategia 85 (Madrid: Institudo de Estudios Estrategicos, May 1996), pp. 37–55; and Jorge Aspizua Turrion, 'La Francia "Atomica"', *Nueva Revista de Politica, Cultura y Arte*, no. 53, September–October 1997, pp. 80–87.

[30] Alfred Cahen, 'La Construction de la Défense Européenne et la Dissuasion Nucléaire', *Relations Internationales et Stratégiques*, no. 21, Spring 1996, pp. 117–20.

[31] For a Polish assessment of the French initiative, see Andrzej Ciupinski, 'Od Odstraszania Francuskiego Do Odstraszania Europejskiego', *Mysl Wojskowa*, no. 3, 1997, pp. 147–56.

[32] Nuclear-weapon issues were discussed by Paris and Bonn on several occasions from the mid-1980s onwards. See Hubert Védrine, *Les Mondes de François Mitterrand; à l'Elysée, 1981–1995* (Paris: Librairie Arthème Fayard, 1996), p. 721.

[33] 'Franco-German Common Concept on Defence and Security', Nuremberg, 9 December 1996.

[34] *Ibid*.

[35] Rühe, interview to television channel ARD.

[36] Paul Quilès, 'La France se Plie à la Volonté des Etats-Unis', *Libération*, 2 February 1997.

[37] See Lothar Rühl, 'Absurde Aufregung', *Die Welt*, 31 January 1997.

[38] Günter Verheugen, interview in *Süddeutsche Zeitung*, 17 July 1997; and 'Concertation Franco-Allemande sur la Dissuasion Nucléaire', *Le Monde*, 13–14 July

1997.

[39] Bozo, 'Dissuasion Concertée', p. 99.

[40] Yves Boyer, 'Les Armes Nucléaires Françaises et l'Europe', *Défense Nationale*, August–September 1996, p. 50.

[41] See Giovanni de Briganti and Theresa Hitchens, 'Skepticism Rains on EU Nuclear Umbrella Idea', *Defense News*, 11–17 September 1995, p. 52.

[42] See Bluth, *Britain, Germany and Western Nuclear Strategy*; Ivo H. Daalder, *The Nature and Practice of Flexible Response: NATO Strategy and Theater Nuclear Forces since 1967* (Ithaca, NY: Cornell University Press, 1991); Beatrice Heuser, *NATO, Britain, France and the FRG: Nuclear Strategies and Forces for Europe, 1949–2000* (London: Macmillan, 1997); and Peters, *The Germans and the INF Missiles*.

[43] 'The Role and Future of Nuclear Weapons', Defence Committee of the WEU Assembly, Document 1,420, 40th Ordinary Session (Part 1), 19 May 1994, p. 28.

[44] Omand, 'Nuclear Deterrence in a Changing World', p. 19.

[45] Article 11 of the Amsterdam Treaty mentions that the goals of the Common Foreign and Security Policy include safeguarding 'the common values, the fundamental interests, the independence and integrity of the Union'.

[46] See Philippe Séguin, 'A Rebuttal: Why France's Nuclear Plan is Serious', *International Herald Tribune*, 6 September 1995.

[47] See Heuser, *NATO, Britain, France and the FRG*, pp. 148–72.

[48] See Mathias Küntzel, *Bonn and the Bomb* (London: Pluto Press, 1995), p. 123; and Elizabeth Young, *The Control of Proliferation: The 1968 Treaty in Hindsight and Forecast*,

Adelphi Paper 56 (London: IISS, 1969).

[49] On early British interest in a European deterrent, see Heuser, *NATO, Britain, France and the FRG*.

[50] Alyson J. K. Bailes, 'A Nuclear-Capable Europe: The Case for the British Deterrent', *Security Dialogue*, vol. 4, no. 3, September 1993, pp. 323–32.

[51] Charles de Gaulle, quoted in Jacques Isnard, 'Le Grand Déballage Nucléaire', *Le Monde*, 4 February 1997.

[52] Edouard Balladur, speech to the Institut des Hautes Etudes de Défense Nationale, Paris, May 1994.

[53] 'Annexe à la Loi No. 96-589', p. 9,988.

[54] Quinlan, *Thinking about Nuclear Weapons*, p. 76.

[55] Beatrice Heuser, 'What Nuclear Strategy for Post-Cold War Europe?', *Orbis*, vol. 36, no. 2, Spring 1992, p. 224.

[56] Kamp, 'Germany and the Future of Nuclear Weapons in Europe', note 18.

[57] 'Antwort der Bundesregierung, Die Zukunft der Britischen und Französischen Nuklearstraitkäfte und ihre Rolle im Kontext einer Europäischen Verteidigungspolitik', *Drucksache 13/7231*, Deutscher Bundestag, 18 March 1997.

[58] David S. Yost, 'Europe and Nuclear Deterrence', *Survival*, vol. 35, no. 3, Autumn 1993, p. 111.

[59] Sloan, *NATO Nuclear Strategy*, p. 9.

[60] Henderson, 'Shaping the UK's Minimum Deterrent'.

[61] See Karl-Heinz Kamp, 'The Future of Nuclear Forces in European Security', paper presented at the Institut Français des Relations Internationales

(IFRI)–SAIC Workshop, 'What Future for Nuclear Forces in International Security?', Paris, 27 February 1992, pp. 16–17.
[62] Frédéric Bozo, 'Une Dissuasion Européenne est-elle Possible?', in *La Communauté, la Défense et la Sécurité Européenne* (Lyon: Centre d'Etude et de Recherche de l'Institut d'Etudes Politiques (CERIEP), 1991), p. 79.
[63] Christopher Mallaby, 'Dissuasion Britannique et Dissuasion Européenne', *Relations Internationales et Stratégiques*, no. 21, Spring 1996, p. 115.
[64] Claudio Virgi, 'L'Europea Integri la Francia Potenza Nucleare', *Il Sole 24 Ore*, 24 November 1995.
[65] Kamp, 'Reshaping Nuclear Europe'.
[66] Pascal Boniface, 'French Nuclear Strategy and European Deterrence: Les Rendez-Vous Manqués', *Contemporary Security Policy*, vol. 17, no. 2, August 1996, p. 234.
[67] See Nicholas Witney, Olivier Debouzy and Robert A. Levine, *Western European Nuclear Forces: A British, a French, and an American View* (Santa Monica, CA: RAND, 1995).

Conclusion

[1] François Heisbourg, *Three Possible Futures: The Role of Nuclear Weapons in International Security – The Next 25 Years*, Future Roles Series Paper 3 (Albuquerque, NM: Sandia National Laboratories, May 1996), p. 16.
[2] Thomas Ender, Holger H. Mey and Michel Rühle, 'The New Germany and Nuclear Weapons', in Garrity and Maaranen (eds), *Nuclear Weapons in the Changing World*, p. 136.
[3] See Slocombe, 'The Future of US Nuclear Weapons'; and Jane Sharp, 'Europe's Nuclear Dominos', *Bulletin of the Atomic Scientists*, June 1993, pp. 29–33.
[4] See Holger Mey, *The Future Role of US Nuclear Weapons in Europe: A German Perspective*, Future Roles Series Paper 8 (Albuquerque, NM: Sandia National Laboratories, January 1997), pp. 10–11.
[5] Sezer, 'Turkey's New Security Environment', p. 162.
[6] Lambert and Miller, *US Nuclear Weapons in Europe*, p. 180.
[7] See Butcher, Nassauer and Young, *Nuclear Futures*.
[8] See Paul M. Cole, *Sweden without the Bomb: The Conduct of a Nuclear-Capable Nation without Nuclear Weapons* (Santa Monica, CA: RAND, 1994).